ROMAN
MYTHOLOGY

JOY PAIGE

rosen central™

The Rosen Publishing Group, Inc., New York

For Scott

Published in 2006 by The Rosen Publishing Group, Inc.
29 East 21st Street, New York, NY 10010

First Edition

Library of Congress Cataloging-in-Publication Data

Paige, Joy.
Roman mythology/Joy Paige.—1st ed.
    p. cm.—(Mythology around the world)
Includes bibliographical references (p.) and index.
ISBN 1-4042-0773-2 (library binding)
1. Mythology, Roman.
I. Title. II. Series.

BL803.P34 2006
292.1'3—dc22

2005010020

Manufactured in the United States of America

On the cover: A Roman fresco of Hercules.

CONTENTS

Introduction   4

1 Daily Life in Rome   6

2 The Origins and Evolution of
   Roman Mythology   16

3 The Mythological Landscape of
   Ancient Rome   23

4 Important Characters in
   Roman Mythology   31

5 The Key Roman Myths   43

   Glossary   57

   For More Information   59

   For Further Reading   61

   Bibliography   61

   Index   63

INTRODUCTION

Often, when people think about mythology, they assume it is simply a trivial literary account of a culture's past. What most people may not realize is that a culture's mythology is a wonderful look into the beliefs and people of that culture. By studying mythology, we learn many important aspects about a civilization, such as its history, religion, and the lives of its people.

The belief in the gods and goddesses that scholars have come to associate with

Roman mythology shaped many aspects of the Romans' daily lives. Romans prayed to their gods each and every day. So why were the ancient Romans consumed and influenced by their mythology? Many historians believe it is because the gods reflected the people's needs in their everyday lives.

Many people believed that the gods had powers that could improve agriculture or bring love, for example. They felt that if the gods were happy, the Romans would be blessed with special gifts. Roman customs, rituals, and holidays were born from a belief in the gods' powers. As such, the history of ancient Rome is woven into its mythology.

To fully understand the importance of Roman mythology, it is necessary to consider the many elements that influenced these beliefs. Some Roman beliefs reflect the history and origins of Roman civilization. The Romans also adopted beliefs from many other cultures, such as that of the Greeks, to form their own mythology. In order to get a better idea of Roman history, it is important to understand the mythology.

1 DAILY LIFE IN ROME

In ancient Rome, different levels of society existed, much the same as today. Some people were wealthy and had many privileges. Others were not as lucky and were considered to be in a lower class. These people were very poor and held jobs that did not allow them to make much money. There were slaves who performed much of the labor in Rome during this time. Children of wealthy families attended primary school, followed by secondary school, and beyond. Male children of slaves went only as far as primary school. The female children of slaves did not go to school at all; many girls were taught at home by their mothers.

Many of the jobs held by Romans were similar to those held by people today. The types of jobs a man could hold depended on his class or status. A wealthy man might be a senator or businessman, spending most of his workday meeting with

Members of the plebian class, such as the old man represented in this first-century BC bust, held common jobs, such as tending to a store or working on a farm.

Novotny and was eventually named the head of the country's Communist party. His reforms during the Prague Spring thrilled many Czechoslovaks but upset Communist leaders in Eastern Europe and the Soviet Union. In August 1968 the Soviet Union led an invasion of Czechoslovakia that forced Dubcek from office.

The following year Dubcek was kicked out of the Communist party leadership and was later forced to work as a forestry official. He was not allowed to talk to anyone except his family without government permission. In 1989 the Czechoslovaks finally ended Communist control of their country. Dubcek was welcomed back into public life and served as the chairman of the country's lawmaking body. On November 7, 1992, he died from injuries suffered during a car accident.

The End of the Prague Spring

The changes in Czechoslovakia alarmed other Communist leaders, especially Gomulka in Poland and Walter Ulbricht in East Germany. Some Soviet leaders also feared that Czechoslovakia's ties to the Warsaw Pact would weaken. This military alliance was controlled by the Soviet Union and included all its Eastern European allies.

Without intending to do so, the media in Czechoslovakia stirred anti-Soviet feelings and began to raise questions about the Warsaw Pact. In May 1968 Soviet premier Aleksei Kosygin visited Dubcek. Vasil Bilak was one of the Czechoslovak Communists who opposed the Prague Spring. He recalled the Soviet message to Dubcek.

> They didn't ask for anything special: just to halt the disintegration of the party, stop anti-Soviet activity and anti-socialist propaganda. Stop the growing voices saying that Czechoslovakia should leave the Warsaw Pact. They said quite openly—"We cannot accept it, we cannot allow the border of the West to come right up to the Soviet border."

In July, Brezhnev met with the leaders of four other Warsaw Pact countries. They discussed how they should restrain the reforms in Czechoslovakia. Brezhnev then met with Dubcek. Stepan Chervonenko, the Soviet ambassador to Czechoslovakia, described the scene: "The situation was quite tense. We came to an agreement that the Czechoslovaks would themselves carry out a certain number of crucial measures to restore order. This involved some changes of personnel, the introduction of tighter control over the mass media, and stricter work among certain layers of society."

Dubcek promised to make the changes Brezhnev wanted, but he acted slowly. Meanwhile, his opponents at home, including Bilak, were asking the Soviet Union to end the "counterrevolution" against communism in Czechoslovakia. On August 3 they passed a secret letter to Brezhnev. In it they wrote that "the very existence of socialism in our country is under threat." They asked the Soviet leadership "to lend support and assistance with all the means at your disposal." Bilak and the others were urging Brezhnev to invade and restore strict Communist rule. The Soviet Union probably would have taken this same action on its own. But now it had an excuse for invading—the faithful Czechoslovak Communists had invited them in.

At 11:00 P.M. on August 20, the Soviet invasion began. Troops from four other Warsaw Pact countries (Hungary, Poland, East Germany, and Bulgaria) also joined the attack. The Czechoslovak citizens offered only slight resistance against this massive force of tanks and 500,000 troops. Some people who opposed the Soviet troops told them to go home or asked why they were carrying out the attack. The soldiers responded that they were just following orders. One order was to arrest Dubcek and bring him to Moscow. In his last radio address, the Czechoslovak leader said, "I ask you please don't be provocative, remain calm, don't let panic take over."

Eduard Goldstucker—a former Czechoslovak diplomat, writer, and supporter of the Prague Spring—compared the

Soviet actions to an earlier invasion of his homeland. Before the start of World War II, Nazi Germany had sent in tanks and troops to take control of Czechoslovakia. Goldstucker said,

> [T]he Soviet invasion in '68 [had an] even crueler impact than the Hitler one...because Hitler was our declared enemy, we didn't expect anything from him but the worst. But here, those who for years and decades preached they're our best friends, our brothers...came with an army of half a million to suppress our drive for a little bit more freedom.

A Soviet tank rolls through Prague during the 1968 Soviet invasion of Czechoslovakia.

The Soviet Union replaced Dubcek with a Communist leader who opposed reform. The Prague Spring led to a bleak winter for the people of Czechoslovakia. Said Havel: "It was a very sad time. People who a year earlier resisted and...put their bodies in front of that overpowering might—these people started to mope, to crouch. They started to fear one another and stopped expressing themselves freely. It was a very demoralizing time."

In the fall of 1968, Leonid Brezhnev explained why the Soviet Union believed it had the right to invade Czechoslovakia. He also stated that the Soviet Union had the right to carry out similar invasions of socialist countries in the future. This policy became known in the West as the "Brezhnev Doctrine." Here are excerpts from an article explaining this doctrine that appeared in *Pravda*, the official newspaper of the Soviet Communist party, in September 1968.

The peoples of the socialist countries and Communist parties certainly do have and should have the freedom for determining the ways of advance of their respective countries.

However, none of their decisions should damage either socialism in their country or the fundamental interests of other socialist countries, and the whole working class movement, which is working for socialism.

This means that each Communist Party is responsible not only to its own peoples, but also to all the socialist countries, to the entire Communist movement. Whoever forgets this, in stressing only the independence of the Communist Party, becomes one-sided. He deviates from his international duty....

It has got to be emphasized that when a socialist country seems to adopt a "non-affiliated" stand, it retains its national independence, in effect, precisely because of the might of the socialist community, and above all the Soviet Union as a central force, which also includes the might of its armed forces. The weakening of any of the links in the world system of socialism directly affects all the socialist countries, which cannot look indifferently at this....

2

GETTING
MAD

Under Leonid Brezhnev, the Soviet Union was not only concerned with supporting Third World countries and asserting its control in Eastern Europe. Adding to its nuclear arsenal was also a major concern. The Cuban Missile Crisis had convinced Soviet leaders that their country could not afford to lose the arms race.

Around the time of the Cuban crisis, the United States had almost four times as many *intercontinental ballistic missiles* (ICBMs) as the Soviet Union had. These long-range missiles could carry nuclear warheads for thousands of miles. The Americans also had ten times as many bombers capable of dropping nuclear bombs. According to Soviet general Valentin Larionov, Soviet leaders became convinced that they had "to catch up and overtake, to try and show everyone that we weren't far behind the Americans, that we too had nuclear weapons."

In 1961, when Nikita Khrushchev was still in power, the Soviet Union had tested the largest *hydrogen bomb* ever. In public Khrushchev said his government hoped it never had to use such a huge bomb during a war. In private he hoped the Americans saw the bomb as a threat. Two years later Soviet, American, and British leaders agreed to stop testing nuclear weapons above the ground and underwater and not to test them in space. But some testing would continue deep below the earth. Under Brezhnev the Soviet Union tested more weapons and built more missiles, trying to catch up to the Americans.

The Bomb   BIG BLAST

In 1960 the Soviet Union and the United States had agreed to halt nuclear weapons testing for a time. The Soviet Union broke that agreement in the summer of 1961. Then in October the Soviet Union stunned the world with a test of the most powerful hydrogen bomb ever. The device set off an explosion equal to 50 *megatons,* or 50 million tons of dynamite. This one *thermonuclear* device had more firepower than all the bombs used during World War II. The flash of light created by the blast could be seen 600 miles (965 km) away.

The Soviet Union tests the largest hydrogen bomb ever.

Mikhail Mokrinski was the pilot of the Soviet plane that dropped the bomb. He described the blast.

We had to put on special glasses, and pull down curtains to protect us against the radiation.... Suddenly there would be something like a rising sun.... Then suddenly there is a huge blow as the shock wave hits the plane, all the controls go crazy, and you have to grab the joystick, and quickly, quickly try and get it under control. The plane was thrown from side to side. We knew what a nuclear explosion was like.

★ The Bomb   ANOTHER NUCLEAR POWER

For years China had asked the Soviet Union to help it build nuclear bombs. In 1957 Khrushchev began giving the Chinese some aid in nuclear technology. Although the Soviet Union ended this assistance in 1959, the Chinese had enough knowledge to continue developing nuclear weapons on their own. Those efforts paid off in 1964. On October 16 China joined the United States, the Soviet Union, Great Britain, and France as members of the nuclear weapons "club." Less than three years later, China tested its first hydrogen bomb.

Mao Zedong, China's leader, seemed less concerned about the dangers of nuclear war than some world leaders. He said, "We may lose more than 300 million people. So what? War is war. The years will pass and we'll get to work producing more babies than before."

The Chinese test did not surprise U.S. leaders. Satellites and U-2 planes had kept them informed of Chinese testing activities. China's nuclear capability was also not an immediate threat to the United States. The Chinese lacked any missile that could reach America. By the 1970s, however, China did have ICBMs that could reach U.S. territory.

Ready for War

In the early 1960s, the United States relied on a diverse nuclear force. It kept missiles underground, in deep holes called *silos*. These silos were spread out in remote areas of the American South and West. The largest of the missiles in these silos was the Titan II, which weighed 150 tons. This ICBM could travel 7,500 miles (12,070 km) and carry a nine-megaton warhead. A smaller ICBM was the Minuteman.

The United States also had nuclear weapons based in countries around the world. Many of these were *tactical weapons*, designed for use on a battlefield. Some of these weapons were stored in countries that belonged to the *North Atlantic Treaty Organization* (NATO). But some nuclear weapons were kept at U.S. military bases in countries that were not part of NATO, such as Japan, South Korea, Spain, and Taiwan. In some cases the governments of the non-NATO countries did not know that U.S. weapons were on their soil.

At sea the United States had submarines that carried long-range nuclear ballistic missiles. These subs roamed the ocean depths, waiting for orders to fire their missiles, sometimes called *submarine-launched ballistic missiles* (SLBMs). Subs based in the Atlantic Ocean alone could fire 144 Polaris missiles in a relatively short period of time.

America's nuclear force in the air was manned by the *Strategic Air Command* (SAC). At any minute of any day, SAC had at least a dozen B-52 bombers in the skies. Each plane carried three or four hydrogen bombs. Each bomb had safety devices, or locks, that prevented them from accidentally blowing up. Other SAC planes were always on alert on the ground, ready to fly in just 15 minutes. Together the SAC planes, SLBMs, and ICBMs were called the triad of America's nuclear force.

The United States also had a defensive system in place. In 1962 the country introduced a Ballistic Missile Early Warning

Radar antennae such as this one were the key element in the Ballistic Missile Early Warning System.

System (BMEWS). This system was designed to detect Soviet missiles long before they reached targets in America or Western Europe. The BMEWS used three radar stations that were linked together. The stations were located in Greenland, Alaska, and England. Tied into a large computer network, the system passed on information about any enemy missile to the *North American Air Defense Command* (NORAD), based in Colorado. Other warning stations were scattered across North America.

The Bomb   THE TITAN II

The Titan II was the first U.S. ICBM that could be fired from underground. A Titan sat in its silo, loaded with fuel, ready to be launched with little warning. Once fired, a Titan could reach the Soviet Union in about 25 to 30 minutes. The warhead on a Titan II was large enough to take out several closely grouped enemy targets.

Titan missile silos were designed to survive a nuclear attack. Inside a silo, U.S. soldiers waited in a control room for instructions to launch their missile. Each crew's members knew their missile would be directed at one of three

possible targets, but they never knew which one until they received specific launch orders. Two crew men had to turn special keys to launch a missile. They had to follow a precise sequence of events before they could use these keys.

Thomas Dency was a crew member at a Titan missile site. He and the other crew members knew that if they received an order to launch, "it was only because...the [Soviet] missiles were already on their way and this was just a way of not letting them maybe take over the entire earth without any obstruction at all. But most of us felt if we did our job right and the Russians knew we were on alert here...that they would not attempt that."

The Birth of MAD

Segment #2 MAD, ABMs, and MIRVs

The policy for using America's vast nuclear force began to change under President John Kennedy. Earlier President Dwight Eisenhower had followed a policy called *massive retaliation.* Any Soviet attack on the United States or its allies would spark a huge U.S. counterattack with nuclear weapons. By 1961, however, the Cold War situation was not the same as it had been during Eisenhower's time. Under Kennedy, Harold Brown was in charge of U.S. weapons technology. Brown said Kennedy had "an understanding that massive retaliation would assure the destruction not only of the Soviet Union but also of the United States and its allies as well, because by that time the Soviet Union had the capability, after such an attack, to respond with a massive nuclear response of its own."

The first change in U.S. policy was announced in 1962 by Secretary of Defense Robert McNamara. In the past, U.S. missiles intended for a possible first strike had been targeted at Soviet cities, as well as military installations. Now, these U.S. nuclear weapons would only be aimed at military targets. The plan was called "No Cities/Counterforce." McNamara hoped the Russians would adopt a similar strategy. Some American generals, however, did not embrace the plan. General Thomas Power was in charge of SAC. He said, "Restraint? Why are you so concerned with saving their lives?

The whole idea is to kill [the Russians]. At the end of the war if there are two Americans and one Russian left alive, we win."

Although Power and other Americans may have talked about winning a nuclear war, some people began thinking that once a nuclear war started, there would be no winners. Said Harold Brown, "If the first day had involved attacks on cities then it would have been just unbelievably catastrophic: tens of millions of deaths and enormous destruction.... World War II killed 50 million people, but it didn't do it in one day."

A new U.S. approach emerged. Some officials believed that the level of U.S. nuclear firepower needed to be large enough to *deter* a Soviet nuclear attack. McNamara later said, "If you want a stable nuclear world...it requires that each side be confident that it can deter the other, and that...requires that there be a balance and the balance is the understanding that if either side initiates the use of nuclear weapons, the other side will respond with sufficient power to inflict unacceptable damage."

This new approach was called *mutual assured destruction.* Some people noticed that together, the first letter of each of these words spelled out MAD. Critics said it was mad to think that it was safer for the Americans to have more weapons than they really needed to destroy the Soviet Union. But McNamara saw MAD as a way to prevent the first use of nuclear weapons.

| Sources | MCNAMARA ON MAD |

In September 1967, just before resigning as secretary of defense, Robert McNamara gave a speech on mutual deterrence—another name for MAD. Here are excerpts from that speech.

The cornerstone of our strategic policy continues to be to deter nuclear attack upon the United States or its allies. We do this by maintaining a highly reliable ability to inflict unacceptable damage upon any single aggressor or combination of aggressors at any time during the course of a strategic nuclear exchange, even after absorbing a surprise first strike. This can be defined as our assured-destruction capability.

It is important to understand that assured destruction is the very essence of the whole deterrence concept. We must possess an actual assured-destruction capability and that capability also must be credible. The point is that a potential aggressor must believe that our assured-destruction capability is in fact actual and that our will to use it in retaliation to an attack is unwavering....

...We must be able to absorb the total weight of nuclear attack on our country...and still be capable of damaging the aggressor to the point that his society would simply no longer be viable in twentieth-century terms. That is what deterrence of nuclear aggression means. It means the certainty of suicide to the aggressor, not merely to his military forces, but to his society as a whole.

Culture — DR. STRANGELOVE

In the mid-1960s, U.S. leaders took MAD seriously. Filmmaker Stanley Kubrick was able to find some humor in the tensions between the United States and the Soviet Union. However, his humor ultimately was bleak. In *Dr. Strangelove, or How I Learned to Stop Worrying and Love the Bomb*, Kubrick shows the beginning of an unplanned nuclear war. Through the film Kubrick makes fun of the people who supported MAD and warns against the dangers of the nuclear era.

The film begins with a crazy SAC commander ordering an unauthorized attack on the Soviet Union. The U.S. president tries to work with the Soviet leader to end the crisis. But one B-52 bomber continues on its mission, threatening to set off a Soviet "Doomsday machine." The machine will trigger a massive nuclear counterattack by the Soviet Union. At the film's end, a crew member on the B-52 sits on a hydrogen bomb as if it were a horse, riding the bomb to its target in the Soviet Union.

Kubrick got his idea for the Doomsday machine from a book written by Herman Kahn, a U.S. nuclear weapons expert. Kahn suggested that a computer could be connected to thousands of H-bombs, which could be set off if the Soviet Union launched a surprise attack. Kahn's idea was never pursued.

The Underwater War

Submarines were increasingly important under MAD. Nuclear-powered subs could remain deep under the ocean's surface for months at time. On U.S. subs, special technology made it almost impossible for Soviet ships to detect them. The U.S. subs carried Polaris missiles. These nuclear weapons were known as "city killers." They were not designed for a first strike on Soviet missile silos. The Polaris missiles would be fired on civilian targets if the Soviet Union ever launched a first strike on U.S. forces.

Joe Williams was a U.S. submarine captain during the early 1960s. He described the role of his sub:

> *It was an extremely survivable, assured-destruction capability that the Soviets knew they could not destroy and knew that if they conducted a first strike, that system would some day be available to retaliate. It might take some time to get the message to them from a destroyed national headquarters, but at some day the missile warheads would come raining in and they would pay the price.*

The Soviet Union also had its own submarine fleet equipped with nuclear weapons. The first of its nuclear-powered subs were built quickly in the late 1950s, during Nikita Khrushchev's rush to match U.S. military might. During a test of one of these subs, an accident on board led to a *radiation* leak that killed at least a dozen crew members. Eventually Soviet engineers perfected their own design for subs that could carry nuclear missiles.

Nikolai Ousenko was the captain of one of the Soviet nuclear subs. He said the tensions of the Cold War and the threat of nuclear war were disturbing. "But we still had to accomplish our task, like the Americans had to accomplish theirs, and we would have accomplished it. What would it have ended in? It would have had very sad consequences for the world."

A U.S. sailor on board a nuclear sub

U.S. submarines had another special role during the Cold War besides the capability to launch nuclear missiles. The navy had a small fleet of subs used for top-secret spy missions. These subs patrolled along the Soviet coast, gathering information on new Soviet ships and subs. Some also had mechanical arms so that they could retrieve objects from the water. The Soviet military sometimes detected these spy subs, but they never captured one.

The first of these subs ran on diesel power. Unlike traditional diesel subs, the spy subs could stay underwater for relatively long periods. They used long pipes called *snorkels* to take in air and carry out engine exhaust while the subs were underwater. Later, nuclear-powered subs allowed for even longer spy missions.

One of the most dangerous activities for the spy subs involved tapping Soviet telephone cables. These cables off the waters of the Soviet Union carried secret military messages. Divers from the spy subs placed special tape recorders on the cables. These recorders picked up the messages being sent through the cables. The subs regularly returned to pick up the tape recordings and take them back to the United States.

Like human spies, the spy subs had to prepare for the chance of being caught. Agents carried poison that they were supposed to use to kill themselves if they were grabbed by enemies. On board the spy subs were explosives. If they were caught, the sailors on board the subs were supposed to blow up their vessels.

Nuclear Risks All Around

Since the 1950s U.S. officials had tried to convince Americans that it was necessary to prepare for a possible nuclear war. *Civil defense* programs, the government said, would help protect people from the dangers of a nuclear blast and its radiation. But in the era of MAD, more people came to believe that civil defense was pointless. Said Harold Brown, "I think the public concluded that if a thermonuclear war were to take place, civil defense, although it might preserve some lives, would not preserve most lives, and what came afterward would have made life not worth living."

Soviet citizens had similar beliefs. The Soviet Union had a massive civil defense program until the late 1980s, but many people doubted its usefulness. Maria Stepanova, a Soviet civil defense worker, said, "[The Russians] used to joke that if a nuclear bomb was dropped nearby all there was left to do was to cover yourself with a white bedsheet and crawl to the cemetery. If you could make it to the cemetery, that is."

Rather than prepare for a nuclear war, some people wanted to prevent one—and end the production of all nuclear weapons. The "Ban the Bomb" movement had begun in the 1950s. One of the largest of the groups opposed to nuclear weapons was the Campaign for Nuclear Disarmament (CND). Started in England in 1958, CND

During the late 1950s, English protesters began an annual march against nuclear weapons.

protested against nuclear arms and tried to influence British politicians. In 1964 it demanded that Great Britain not buy U.S. Polaris missiles. British leaders ignored this demand, and CND slowly lost influence. The Soviet Union, however, both openly and secretly supported Western groups that opposed nuclear weapons. Some of these groups also received secret Soviet funds. Any efforts to reduce missiles used by the West were welcomed by the Soviet government.

The dangers of nuclear weapons went beyond all-out war. Accidents with these weapons happened throughout the late

1950s and 1960s. In 1961 a B-52 bomber carrying nuclear bombs broke apart in midair over North Carolina. One of the weapons fell to earth and was never found. Seven years later a B-52 with nuclear bombs on board crashed near Thule, Greenland. The bombs did not explode, but some radiation was released. The Soviet Union most likely had similar accidents, though the West never learned of them.

Places   PALOMARES, SPAIN

Palomares, Spain, is a small town on the Mediterranean Sea. For a few months in 1966, Palomares was the site of an intense hunt for a "broken arrow"—the U.S. nickname for a lost or damaged nuclear bomb.

On January 17 a B-52 bomber collided in midair with a tanker plane. Four hydrogen bombs fell from the plane and landed near Palomares. Safety devices prevented the bombs from exploding, but some *radioactive plutonium* did leak out. At first the U.S. government denied that the B-52 had been carrying nuclear weapons, but then it admitted the truth. Three of the bombs were quickly found on land, but a fourth landed somewhere in the Mediterranean.

For 80 days U.S. ships sealed off the area and searched for the lost bomb. It was finally recovered on April 7. In the meantime, the people of Palomares had been warned not to eat certain foods or

This "broken arrow" was recovered off the coast of Spain in 1966.

go near certain areas. The bombs' plutonium posed a threat to their safety. The U.S. government removed 1,700 tons of contaminated soil from the village. The soil was taken to America in barrels and buried.

About 20 years after the incident, some people in Palomares still had traces of plutonium in their bodies. Experts disagreed on the health dangers posed by those levels of the substance.

Missiles Against Missiles

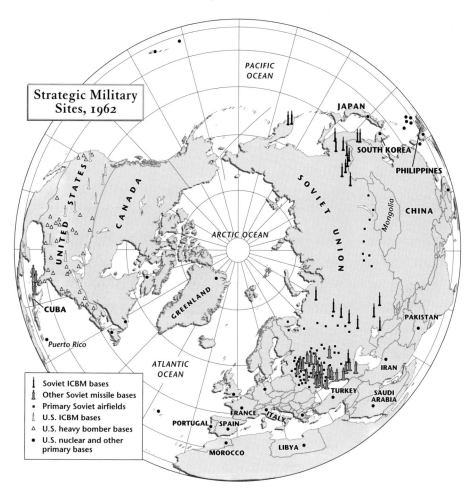

Strategic Military Sites, 1962

- Soviet ICBM bases
- Other Soviet missile bases
- Primary Soviet airfields
- U.S. ICBM bases
- U.S. heavy bomber bases
- U.S. nuclear and other primary bases

By 1967 the Soviet Union had almost caught up to the United States in the production of nuclear missiles. The Soviet Union had more than 400 missiles, including the SS-9, which could hit a target 7,000 miles (11,265 km) away. Soviet military forces were also working on a new goal: a defensive system to stop U.S. missiles from reaching the Soviet Union. The designers developed missiles that could blow up U.S. missiles while they were in the air. These defensive missiles were called *antiballistic missiles* (ABMs).

The Americans were worried about the Soviet plans for an ABM system. Using such a system would upset the balance of MAD. Said William Lee, a U.S. defense analyst, MAD "must be mutual, and it must be assured. So anything on either side that would interfere with...either side's capability to kill 20 to 50 percent of the population of the other side is, by definition, destabilizing."

These concerns did not stop the United States from working on its own ABM system. But Secretary of Defense McNamara was reluctant to put it in place. The system was too expensive and not foolproof. He convinced President Johnson to meet with Soviet leaders and propose that neither side introduce ABMs.

In June 1967 Johnson met in Glassboro, New Jersey, with Soviet premier Aleksei Kosygin. Johnson made his case for not using ABMs. Kosygin did not accept the argument. The Soviet Union wanted to talk about reducing the number of offensive weapons. The meeting ended with no agreements, and Soviet leaders went ahead with their plan to put an ABM system around Moscow.

Meanwhile, U.S. scientists were working on a new offensive threat: *multiple independently targeted reentry vehicles* (MIRVs). Now, one missile could carry ten separate warheads that could be aimed at ten different targets. A number of MIRVs could be launched at Moscow and overwhelm the ABM system. The Soviet Union would have to spend huge amounts of money to try to defend itself. Said Nikolai Detinov, a Soviet defense official, "The Soviet Union realized that...the Americans, who were financially better off, could out-do the Soviet Union.... [N]ow we had to choose between building...communism, or making missiles."

In the summer of 1968, Soviet and U.S. officials announced their plan to meet and discuss limiting both offensive and defensive missiles. The first meeting was scheduled for September 1968, but it was postponed after the Soviet invasion of Czechoslovakia in August. The first talks did not take place until November 1969. The meetings were known as the *Strategic Arms Limitation Talks* (SALT). Richard Nixon was now the U.S. president. His chief advisor on foreign policy and national security was Henry Kissinger. These two men and their Soviet counterparts began the long process of slowing down the arms race.

3

THE
RISE
OF
DÉTENTE

During his political career, Richard Nixon was always strongly anti-Communist. After his presidency he wrote, "Never once in my career have I doubted the Communists mean it when they say their goal is to bring the world under Communist control." But Nixon also believed that it was better to communicate with Soviet and Chinese leaders than to ignore them. Early in his presidency, Nixon said, "I felt that the relationship between the United States and the Soviet Union would probably be the single most important factor in determining whether the world would live at peace during and after my administration."

Preventing nuclear conflict was not Nixon's only goal. During his campaign for president, he had promised to end the war in Vietnam. Nixon hoped that by improving relations with the Soviet Union, Moscow would pressure the North Vietnamese to end the war.

On the Soviet side, Leonid Brezhnev also had an interest in dealing with the Americans. The Soviet leader had been through World War II. One of his advisors, Georgi Arbatov, said Brezhnev "returned [from the war] with the very strong conviction that he had to do his best to prevent war." Added Soviet ambassador Anatoly Dobrynin, "Whether the West believed it or not, our attitude was to have a more constructive relationship with the United States." This easing of tension between the two Cold War opponents was called détente.

People ☭ ANATOLY DOBRYNIN

For almost 25 years, Anatoly Dobrynin served in Washington, D.C., as the Soviet ambassador to the United States. He lived through and was personally involved in some of the worst moments of the Cold War. Dobrynin also played a part in helping his country and the United States develop better relations.

Dobrynin was born in Krasnaya Gorka, Ukraine, on November 16, 1919. In 1944 he was working as an aviation engineer when he was recruited to join the Soviet foreign service. During the 1950s he worked at the Soviet embassy in Washington and was part of the Soviet delegation to the United Nations (UN). In 1962 Soviet leader Nikita Khrushchev made Dobrynin the Soviet ambassador to the United States.

Just a few months after taking his new job, Dobrynin became involved in the Cuban Missile Crisis. His late-night meetings with Attorney General Robert Kennedy led to an agreement between the two sides. After that, U.S. officials often came to Dobrynin to discuss secretly their concerns with the Soviet Union. His meetings with Henry Kissinger helped bring about the first SALT treaty. Dobrynin later reflected on the process started by SALT: "[F]or the first time in history, we stopped to think about how first to control the weapons, then to limit them, and then to destroy them. And I hope that this process will carry on."

Dobrynin served in Washington until 1986, when Soviet leader Mikhail Gorbachev appointed him to a senior post in Moscow. After officially retiring in 1988, Dobrynin served as a consultant on foreign affairs.

Talks Through the "Back Channel"

The first formal SALT talks began in November 1969 in Helsinki, Finland. The Americans wanted to focus on ABMs. The Soviet delegates concentrated more on offensive weapons. Problems arose as the two sides tried to define their terms and decide how limits would be enforced. For example, the Soviet Union wanted to include limits on weapons based in

"Wien"—Vienna—was the site of 1970 SALT talks between U.S. and Soviet officials.

NATO countries and the United States. Raymond Garthoff was a U.S. arms expert. In his view Soviet leaders "didn't much see the difference between a one-megaton warhead coming in an ICBM from the United States or a one-megaton warhead hitting that same target delivered by a fighter bomber that had taken off from a base in Turkey." However, the Americans wanted to limit only weapons based in the United States.

As the talks dragged on, the Soviet Union continued its missile production. In some categories it now had more weapons than the United States. America was also spending large sums of money to fight in Vietnam. Nixon and Kissinger felt added pressure to reach an arms agreement. They decided to take a new approach to negotiating with the Soviet Union. They used what was called a "back channel." While teams of diplomats met publicly, Kissinger held private talks with Ambassador Dobrynin. Said Dobrynin, "These meetings made it possible to introduce corrections or amendments without losing face. Using the back channel...we could first state the official point of view, and then talk more freely."

Soviet missiles are paraded through Moscow's Red Square.

In May 1971 the Soviets and Americans announced some of their agreements on nuclear weapons. Both sides would limit their ABM systems. The United States was also willing to discuss limiting the number of SLBMs. A few months later, President Nixon said he would travel to the Soviet Union in 1972 for a meeting with Brezhnev. Détente seemed to be working. Outside events also affected the process.

While talking with Moscow, Nixon and Kissinger were trying to improve relations with China, as well. Kissinger had opened another back channel with the Chinese, preparing the way for Nixon to visit their Communist leaders. China and the Soviet Union had once been close allies, but their relations had soured in the late 1950s. Nixon and Kissinger thought that better U.S. relations with China would make the Soviet Union more willing to deal with the United States in the SALT talks. The Soviet Union would not want China to have better relations with the United States than it had.

In February 1972 Nixon became the first U.S. president to visit Communist China. The meeting stirred some fear in the Soviet Union. "It was a great scare for our leaders," said Arbatov, "who decided that an anti-Soviet coalition was being formed, which included not only America and NATO but also China. We felt we were being surrounded."

Nixon's trip had done what he and Kissinger had hoped it would: push forward the arms talks with Moscow. After Nixon returned from China, Kissinger made a secret trip to Moscow. He and Brezhnev made final agreements on the SALT treaty. Nixon then prepared for his trip to Moscow. Events in Vietnam, however, almost derailed the summit meeting.

People   **WILLY BRANDT**

While American and Soviet officials discussed SALT, Willy Brandt was pursuing his own policy of détente. In October 1969 Brandt became chancellor of West Germany. He immediately recognized East Germany as a separate state. Until then West German leaders had refused to accept the existence of East Germany. Brandt also improved West Germany's relations with the

Soviet Union. His strategy was called *Ostpolitik*—German for "eastern policy."

Brandt was born on December 16, 1913, in Lubeck, Germany. His real name was Herbert Frahm. He changed it to Willy Brandt in 1933, after joining a socialist group that opposed Adolf Hitler and his Nazi government. The Nazis later stripped Brandt of his German citizenship, but he regained it after World War II.

In 1949 Brandt was elected to West Germany's first parliament. He later served as mayor of West Berlin. In 1961 he urged the United States to protest the Berlin Wall. Later, however, Brandt came to believe it was better to work with the East Germans and the Soviet Union than to force a confrontation. This view shaped his Ostpolitik when he became chancellor. In 1970 Brandt became the first West German chancellor to visit East Germany. He later visited the Soviet Union and Poland.

At first the United States had doubts about Brandt's Ostpolitik. But then Nixon and Kissinger saw value in it—as long as the U.S. role in West Berlin would not be affected. Brandt's diplomatic efforts won him the 1971 Nobel Peace Prize. He remained involved in German politics until his death on October 8, 1992.

Signing the SALT Accords

In April 1972 the United States began a new, massive military campaign against North Vietnam. Kissinger worried that the Soviet Union might cancel Nixon's trip. However, Nixon was willing to bet that Soviet leaders would still hold the summit meeting, even after the American moves in Vietnam. The president was right. On May 22 Nixon became the first active U.S. president to visit the Kremlin, the seat of the Soviet government. Dobrynin later said that Soviet leaders were angry with Nixon about Vietnam. But "Brezhnev realized that if he gave way to his emotions, he could undermine what had already been achieved, because the nuclear issues had already been settled...."

On May 26 Brezhnev and Nixon signed the first SALT accords. The two sides formally agreed to limit ABMs. Each side would have just two of these anti-missile systems. SALT I, as the agreement became known, also limited each side to the current number of ICBMs and SLBMs it already had or was building. The Soviet Union had more of each, though the Americans had more warheads for their missiles. Warheads themselves were not restricted. Overall, Soviet leaders were pleased: For the first time, the United States had recognized the Soviet Union as its equal as a superpower. Nixon and Kissinger were also happy since SALT had slowed the arms race.

During their summit meeting, Nixon and Brezhnev signed an agreement describing the basic relations between their countries. They acknowledged a need for both states to "do their utmost to avoid military confrontations and to prevent the outbreak of nuclear war." The two sides also made trade agreements and plans for a joint space mission.

Nixon received some criticism for the SALT accords. Some Americans did not want to deal with the Russians or possibly limit U.S. military might. But Nixon assured the country, "No power on earth is stronger than the United States of America today. And none will be stronger than the United States of America in the future."

Problems at Home and Abroad

After signing the SALT I accords, the Americans and the Soviets began a new round of arms talks called SALT II. At home, however, Richard Nixon was running into trouble. The Watergate scandal was weakening his leadership. Watergate involved a 1972 break-in at the headquarters of the Democratic party, carried out by men working for Nixon. After the break-in became news, Nixon made the situation worse by trying to hide his knowledge of it.

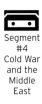
Still, détente went on, though a new crisis in the Middle East threatened to end it. In October 1973, on the Jewish holy day of Yom Kippur, Egypt and Syria launched a surprise attack against Israel. Once again the United States supported the Israelis and the Soviet Union backed the Arabs. The two superpowers sent in supplies to their allies, though they also called for an end to the war. The Arabs took the first advantage in the war, but the Israelis fought back. On October 14 their forces beat the Egyptians in the world's largest tank battle since World War II.

An Israeli flag flies on the east bank of the Suez Canal after the land was recaptured by Israeli forces during the 1973 Yom Kippur War.

Shortly after this Israeli victory, the two sides agreed to a cease-fire, which Kissinger and Brezhnev helped negotiate. Then, the Israelis broke the cease-fire, which upset Moscow. Brezhnev sent a note to Nixon warning that if the two superpowers together could not stop the Israelis, the Soviet Union would act on its own.

U.S. officials then put American military forces on a worldwide nuclear alert—the highest since the Cuban Missile Crisis of 1962. But Brezhnev did not take action against Israel, and the crisis ended when the United States convinced Israel to accept another cease-fire. The Yom Kippur War led to tense moments, but both the Soviet Union and the United States were eager to avoid a Cold War conflict over the Middle East.

Soon after the war, in 1974, Kissinger again traveled to Moscow to continue discussions on arms reduction. By then Kissinger was the U.S. secretary of state. He was virtually running U.S. foreign policy on his own, since President Nixon was so involved with Watergate. In August the growing scandal led Congress to consider impeaching Nixon. He resigned before impeachment took place. Gerald Ford became the new president, and he tried to continue détente with the Russians.

Sources ☆　ONGOING ARMS TALKS

U.S. and Soviet leaders spent many hours holding private talks about nuclear arms reduction. In March 1974 Leonid Brezhnev and Henry Kissinger met in Moscow. Here are excerpts from one of their conversations on nuclear arms.

Brezhnev: *If we let our purely military men into this sphere we'll end up with an unprecedented arms race.... [T]here is the secretary of defense saying the United States has to be militarily stronger. And there are others in the United States echoing these views.... Surely, Dr. Kissinger, if we let ourselves be carried away by that kind of talk, all our discussions will come to nothing....*

Kissinger: *Mr. General Secretary, the entire policy of this administration is based on the presupposition that neither side can achieve military superiority over the other and should not attempt to achieve military superiority over the other. If either tries to talk to the other from a position of strength, it will be a disaster for our two peoples and for all mankind.... [O]f course our people are also watching Soviet developments, and as the Soviet Union develops new weapons, they are used as a justification for our new weapons.... According to our estimate, you're developing four new missiles....*

Brezhnev: *...I can say we're not making a single new missile. We're improving our missiles.*

Kissinger: *It's just a question of definition. It's such a great improvement that to our people it looks like a new one. But I won't debate it. But we're not saying it's in violation of the agreement.*

Brezhnev: *Let us not proceed from what people think but from official statements of governments, and from what lends itself to control.*

Kissinger: *I agree.*

Détente Under Ford

Soon after Gerald Ford took office, he traveled to Vladivostok in the Soviet Union to meet with Brezhnev. The two leaders tried to set guidelines for how SALT II should proceed. Ford later said he thought "Mr. Brezhnev was more anxious than his military advisors to achieve some nuclear understanding." Ford's own military officials felt the same as their Soviet counterparts.

But Ford left Vladivostok confident that he had made real progress on arms control. He and Brezhnev agreed to limit the total number of delivery vehicles for nuclear weapons at 2,400 apiece. The two sides also decided that neither country could equip more than 1,320 missiles with MIRVs. Still, Ford and Brezhnev did have some disagreements. The Soviet Union wanted to include a proposed U.S. missile, the cruise missile, as a delivery vehicle, while the Americans wanted to include a new Soviet plane, the Backfire. Each side refused the other's condition. The issues were left open for later discussion.

Despite Ford's positive feelings about the new agreements, some U.S. leaders were upset that America was pursuing détente.

They first wanted the Soviet Union to recognize the human rights of its citizens. Senator Henry "Scoop" Jackson, a Democrat from Washington, led the criticism of SALT and Soviet policies. He was particularly concerned about the free movement of Soviet Jews. Many of these people were trying to leave the Soviet Union for Israel, but the Soviet government refused to let them go. Jackson said, "When we have something we feel strongly about—and in this case it is civil liberties and freedom…we should put that issue of principle on the table.…"

Soviet leader Leonid Brezhnev and U.S. president Gerald Ford prepare to shake hands after completing a round of discussions in Helsinki, Finland.

Human rights became an issue soon after Jackson spoke. In the summer of 1975, representatives from the United States, Canada, the Soviet Union, and 32 other European countries met in Helsinki, Finland, at the Conference on Security and Cooperation. They drafted a document that became known as the Helsinki Accords. The document had three sections. The first confirmed the existing borders in Europe. The second called for improving trade and scientific and cultural exchanges between the countries. The third—and most controversial—called for all the governments signing the accords to respect the human rights of their citizens.

Some Americans opposed recognizing the European borders created after World War II. These new borders favored the Soviet Union in Eastern Europe. But Ford and other U.S. leaders welcomed the section on human rights. Said Ford, "We the United States believed that if we could get the Soviet Union and the Warsaw Pact nations to respect human rights, that was worth whatever else was agreed to in the Helsinki Accords."

However, some Soviet leaders had a very different reaction to the last section of the accords. Ambassador Dobrynin said, "The members of the [party leadership] read the full text.... When they got to the third 'humanitarian' article, their hair stood on end." Brezhnev had to convince these doubters to accept the whole agreement. He said, "We are masters in our own house, and we shall decide what we implement and what we ignore." Both superpowers signed the Helsinki Accords, but the section on human rights would play a part in future U.S.-Soviet relations.

Technology   DÉTENTE IN SPACE

In 1969 the United States came out ahead in the space race when astronauts Neil Armstrong and Buzz Aldrin became the first humans to walk on the moon. But in 1975 the Soviet Union and the United States tried cooperating in space. The Apollo-Soyuz Test Project (ASTP) came out of the SALT agreement signed in 1972. It was supposed to test technologies that could be used by both sides to make rescues in outer space. On July 15, 1975, a Soviet Soyuz spacecraft blasted off with cosmonauts Aleksei Leonov and Valery Kubasov on board. Later that day, the Americans launched an Apollo spacecraft carrying astronauts Thomas Stafford, Deke Slayton, and Vance Brand. Two days later the two craft met up about 140 miles (225 km) above Earth.

The Apollo capsule had a special docking module attached to its front. The Soyuz then maneuvered into the dock. A few hours later, Leonov left his capsule and entered the Apollo craft. He greeted the Americans in English; they replied in Russian. The astronauts exchanged gifts and shared a meal. During the next two days, they conducted five experiments together.

The ASTP marked the first time that astronauts from different countries met and worked together in space. However, some Americans criticized the mission, saying it was too expensive and did not produce any meaningful technical knowledge. Still, ASTP was a powerful sign of détente. Said astronaut Brand, "I think the biggest benefit for us and possibly the world was that it was a foot in the door for us for better communications between the two countries. We served as an example in the middle of this very unfriendly Cold War...that both sides could put everything into [a joint effort] and make it work."

This image shows the Apollo (left) and Soyuz spacecraft preparing to dock in space.

In 1961 Aleksandr Solzhenitsyn wrote the novel *One Day in the Life of Ivan Denisovich*. The book drew on Solzhenitsyn's experiences in a labor camp, or *gulag*, during the rule of Joseph Stalin. Solzhenitsyn had been arrested in 1945 after writing a letter critical of Stalin and his policies. He was released in 1953.

Stalin's successor, Nikita Khrushchev, was eager to expose some of the abuses committed under Stalin—as long as none of the revealed information made Khrushchev look bad. He allowed the literary journal *Novy Mir* to publish Solzhenitsyn's book. *Denisovich* showed the brutality of the gulags. It created a sensation within the Soviet Union and around the world.

Soon after, Khrushchev withdrew his support for Solzhenitsyn and his writings. The author became a leading *dissident*—a critic of the Communist system. His writings were often banned in the Soviet Union, though still published in the West. In 1970 Solzhenitsyn won the Nobel Prize for Literature, but Soviet authorities continued to harass him. He wrote an acceptance speech in honor of his Nobel prize, but never gave the speech. He feared that if he went to Sweden to accept the prize, he would not be allowed back into the Soviet Union. In his speech Solzhenitsyn wrote, "Woe to that nation whose literature is disturbed by the intervention of power. Because that is not just a violation against freedom of print. It is the closing down of the heart of the nation...."

Solzhenitsyn turned from fiction to nonfiction, writing a detailed work about the gulags. His manuscript for *The Gulag Archipelago* was taken by the KGB in 1973. Solzhenitsyn decided to have the book published in Paris. Early in 1974 the Soviet government took away his citizenship and banished him from the country.

To American critics of détente, the campaign against Solzhenitsyn was proof that the Soviet Union did not respect human rights. Solzhenitsyn became a hero in the West. Solzhenitsyn, however, did not like Western democracy any more than he supported Soviet communism. He settled in Switzerland, then eventually moved to Vermont. In 1990 the Soviet government restored his citizenship. Four years later Solzhenitsyn returned to Russia.

4

RETURN TO CONFLICT

During Angola's 1975 civil war, members of the Popular Movement for the Liberation of Angola (MPLA) pose with their weapons.

Détente under President Ford was not always smooth. Even as the joint Apollo-Soyuz mission was underway, the Soviet Union and the United States were playing out a Cold War confrontation in Angola. A former colony of Portugal, this African country received its independence in 1975. Rival groups then struggled to gain control of the country.

The United States supported the National Front for the Liberation of Angola (FNLA), an anti-Communist organization. The Americans also supported the National Union for the Total Independence of Angola (UNITA), a group that had formerly been part of the FNLA. The Soviet Union and Cuba backed a pro-Communist group, the Popular Movement for the Liberation of Angola (MPLA).

The United States, through the *Central Intelligence Agency* (CIA), sent millions of dollars worth of supplies and arms to its favored groups. The Soviet Union had been giving the MPLA money since the 1960s. Now, it increased its aid. Fidel Castro of Cuba also sent thousands of his soldiers to fight with the MPLA. He acted on his own, not on orders from Brezhnev, but Soviet leaders strongly backed Cuba's participation. The Soviet Union provided aircraft to transport the Cubans to Angola.

The Americans were not pleased. They saw the Cubans as a *proxy*, or a country acting in place of another country or group— in this case, the Soviet Union. Said Secretary of State Kissinger, "[I]f the Soviet Union could intervene at such distances from areas that were far from the traditional Russian security concerns, and when Cuban forces could be introduced into distant trouble spots, and if the West could not find a counter to that...then the whole international system could be destabilized."

Late in 1975 the United States found its own proxy to fight in Angola, secretly encouraging South Africa to send troops to fight the MPLA. The South Africans had their own reasons to get involved—they feared that Communists would launch attacks on their country from Angola if the MPLA gained power. But U.S. aid and South African troops were not enough to stop the MPLA.

Early in 1976 the U.S. Senate voted to stop sending aid to the FNLA and UNITA. President Ford attacked the move, saying it would "have the gravest consequences for the long-term position of the United States and for international order in general; a great nation cannot escape its responsibilities." Neither the United States nor the Soviet Union was ready to end the war of ideology and the struggle for global influence.

Places ANGOLA

Angola is located on Africa's southwest coast. Its capital is Luanda. In the 16th century, Portuguese slave traders came to the area. They worked with local tribes to send African slaves to the Portuguese colony of Brazil. Angola became Portugal's largest and wealthiest African colony.

In 1961 the MPLA began a civil war to gain Angola's independence. UNITA and other groups also joined this struggle. They had a common goal of ending Portuguese rule, but otherwise these rebel groups usually did not cooperate. In 1974 new leaders in Portugal finally began making plans to grant Angola its independence. The various rebel groups then began their struggle for power, receiving U.S. and Soviet help.

Late in 1975 the MPLA gained control of Luanda and declared itself the ruler of an independent Angola. Fighting continued between the new government and UNITA, which was led by Jonas Savimbi. Cuban troops remained in Angola until 1991 to help fight Savimbi's forces. Elections were held the next year, but the civil war continued. UNITA and the government signed a peace treaty in 1994. By then hundreds of thousands of Angolan civilians had been killed or had fled the country to avoid the bloodshed. The UN sent in troops to try to preserve the peace, but by 1998 fighting had resumed.

The Search for Deeper Cuts

In November 1976 Jimmy Carter defeated Gerald Ford for the U.S. presidency. Carter was the first Democrat to hold the office since Lyndon Johnson in 1968. Unlike Johnson, however, Carter was a newcomer to national politics. No one knew how he would handle U.S. foreign affairs, particularly with the Soviet Union. He had already sent mixed messages about his approach. Carter said he wanted to reduce defense spending and promised "no more Vietnams." But he also felt that the Soviet Union had been getting the best out of détente. "We have been outtraded in almost every instance," he said.

When he was sworn in as president in January 1977, Carter said his "ultimate goal [was] the elimination of all nuclear weapons from earth." He appointed Cyrus Vance secretary of state. Vance wanted to work with the Soviet Union whenever possible. But

Zbigniew Brzezinski was national security advisor under Jimmy Carter.

Carter also received advice from a strong anti-Communist, National Security Advisor Zbigniew Brzezinski. Said one American diplomat, Vance always played by the rules of diplomacy, but Brzezinski "was more of a street fighter."

Shortly after Carter took office, he sent Vance to Moscow to discuss arms reductions. Carter wanted to make deep cuts in nuclear weapons. He proposed the two sides go beyond the agreements Ford and Brezhnev had made in 1974. Moscow refused. Said Ambassador Dobrynin, "Our position was very simple: We thought everything had been agreed in Vladivostok." Carter later sensed that he had made a mistake by challenging Brezhnev to make even deeper cuts so soon after the Vladivostok talks.

People   JIMMY CARTER

To his critics Jimmy Carter was a peanut farmer who was overwhelmed by the demands of being U.S. president. To his supporters Carter was a deeply religious man who tried to introduce morality to world affairs. Despite some successes, Carter's four years in office were a difficult time for him and the United States.

James Earl Carter was born on October 1, 1924, in Plains, Georgia. A graduate of the U.S. Naval Academy, he spent many years serving on submarines. When he returned to Georgia, Carter took over the family peanut business and then entered politics. In 1970 he was elected governor of his home state. When he entered the 1976 presidential race, Carter was almost unknown outside Georgia. But he impressed voters with his honesty. And after the scandals of the Nixon years, Americans were ready for a leader who was a Washington "outsider" and a Democrat.

Once in office, Carter had many problems. The economy was struggling. He and Congress had poor relations, and Carter was unable to pass some of his major policies. In foreign affairs his stress on human rights angered the Soviet Union. Even some U.S. allies thought this policy was not productive. Carter was also embarrassed by the Iranian hostage crisis that began late in 1979. Iranian protesters, supported by their government, took over the U.S. embassy in Tehran, Iran. The takeover came after Carter allowed the former leader of Iran—Mohammed Reza Shah Pahlavi—into the United States for medical treatment. More than 50 Americans were kept as hostages in Iran for the last 15 months of Carter's presidency.

Carter did achieve some positive goals. He helped negotiate a historic peace treaty between Israel and Egypt. Known as the Camp David Accords, the agreement was the first of its kind between Israel and one of its Arab neighbors. Carter also started formal diplomatic relations with Communist China and signed the SALT II treaty with the Soviet Union. But many Americans saw Carter's presidency as a failure. After leaving office Carter continued to work for human rights and democracy around the world.

Sources   A LETTER TO BREZHNEV

During his first week as president, Jimmy Carter sent a letter to Soviet leader Leonid Brezhnev. In it Carter outlined some of his views on U.S.-Soviet relations. Here are excerpts from that letter.

I want to confirm that my aim is to improve relations with the Soviet Union on the basis of reciprocity, mutual respect and advantage.... I read your public statements with great interest and they make me believe that we share a common aspiration for strengthening and preserving the perspectives for stable peace.

As I understand your highly important speech in Tula, the Soviet Union will not strive for superiority in arms, it will stand against such a conception, and...it will require only a defense which is strong enough to deter any potential enemy. The United States does not want anything less or more for itself. Therefore, our two countries, with consistency and wisdom, should be able to avoid a new arms race....

At the same time, we cannot be indifferent to the fate of freedom and individual human rights. We represent different social systems, and our countries differ from each other in their history and experience. A competition in ideals and ideas is inevitable between our societies. Yet this must not interfere with common efforts toward formation of a more peaceful, just and humane world....

Human Rights in the Communist Bloc

The failure of Vance's mission to Moscow to attain sharp nuclear weapons reductions put an immediate strain on the U.S. relationship with the Soviet Union. Other problems soon followed. Carter put a heavy emphasis on human rights, and he supported Soviet and Eastern European dissidents who challenged the Communist system. Said Carter, "I was very convinced before I became president that...the end of abuse by governments of their people was a...basic principle on which the United States should be an acknowledged champion." Supporting human rights was not just a moral issue. Brzezinski thought it had political value, too: "[R]aising the issue of human rights pointed to one of the fundamental weaknesses of the Soviet system, namely that it was a system based on oppression."

Segment #5 Human Rights Behind the Iron Curtain

Under Carter the U.S. State Department backed Charter 77, a Czechoslovak group formed to keep track of human rights violations. The United States also supported various Helsinki Watch groups. Named for the Helsinki Accords, these were other groups set up to monitor human rights in Communist countries. Under the accords, the Soviet Union had agreed to respect human rights. Prominent dissidents took part in these monitoring efforts. In Czechoslovakia playwright Vaclav Havel was a part of Charter 77.

Soviet nuclear physicist Andrei Sakharov was also involved in human rights efforts. Sakharov had once been a hero for his work on the hydrogen bomb. However, his dissident views led the Soviet government to banish him from Moscow to the city of Gorky. Another Soviet dissident was Dr. Anatoly Koryagin. He was jailed after he talked about the brutal treatment of other dissidents in mental hospitals. The Soviet government sometimes declared that its political opponents were mentally ill and sent them to these hospitals. One dissident described her experience in a hospital: "They gave us handfuls of drugs three times a day so the body couldn't stand it anymore.... I couldn't speak. My whole mouth and jaw were paralyzed. My tongue was swollen. My arms and legs were shaking."

Another group of dissidents was made up of Soviet Jews who wanted to leave the country. Their struggle had become a political issue a few years earlier. They received even more attention under Carter's policy of promoting human rights. The Jews who could not leave the Soviet Union were called "refuseniks." Many were treated as political enemies and sent to prison camps. One of the most famous refuseniks was Anatoly Shcharansky. In 1978 he was sent to a gulag. He remained there until 1986, when he emigrated to Israel. There he became an Israeli politician known as Natan Sharansky. In the West his case was a symbol of the oppression practiced in the Soviet Union. All the Soviet abuses of human rights eroded the spirit of détente.

Sources   CHARTER 77

In January 1977 more than 200 Czechoslovaks formed Charter 77 to promote human rights in their country. Here are excerpts from the document that they signed outlining their concerns. Soon after this document was released, the Czechoslovak government began arresting many of the dissidents who signed it.

[The publication of laws relating to the Helsinki Accords] serves as a powerful reminder of the extent to which basic human rights in our country exist, regrettably, on paper alone.

...Tens of thousands of our citizens are prevented from working in their own fields for the sole reason that they hold views differing from official ones, and are discriminated against and harassed in all kinds of ways by the authorities and public organizations....

Hundreds of thousands of other citizens are...being condemned to the constant risk of unemployment or other penalties if they voice their own opinions.

...Countless young people are prevented from studying because of their own views or even their parents'. Innumerable citizens live in fear of their own or their children's right to education being withdrawn if they should ever speak up in accordance with their own convictions....

Charter 77 is a loose, informal, and open association of people...united by the will to strive individually and collectively for the respecting of civil and human rights in our own country and throughout the world....

New Missiles, East and West

Talks to limit nuclear weapons continued, but at the same time, both sides were preparing new weapons. The Soviet Union moved first. In 1977 it introduced the SS-20 missile. The range of this missile was not long enough for its production to be limited by SALT I. But to the Americans and their allies in NATO, the SS-20 missile seemed to pose a new threat. The SS-20 was an *intermediate-range missile*. Both the United States and the Soviet Union relied mostly on long-range ICBMs for their nuclear force. The Americans believed the new missiles were targeted on Europe.

Brzezinski summed up the concern about the new missiles: "[T]he SS-20, while perhaps not a decisive military weapon, posed the risk of decoupling Europe's security from America's; namely of posing before us the dilemma that maybe Europe was threatened by nuclear devastation, but that we were not, and therefore should we risk the devastation of our own people and our own cities in order to protect Europe?"

Carter felt pressure from some Americans and Europeans to respond quickly to this new possibility. Carter took what was called a "twin track" with the Soviet Union. He proposed arms control talks to limit intermediate-range missiles, but he also called for new American missiles in Europe to counter the SS-20s. He boosted defense spending and began to expand U.S. conventional forces, as well.

The new U.S. missiles were also intermediate-range weapons: the Pershing II ballistic missile and the cruise missile. The Pershing was an update of an older model, while the cruise missile used new technology. Carter proposed putting 108 Pershings in Germany, while 464 cruise missiles would go to various NATO countries. The missile plan was supported by Western European governments, but it stirred criticism in some quarters.

Technology ☆ THE SS-20

The Soviet Union took a big step forward in its missile technology with the SS-20. Also known as the Saber, the new missile replaced the SS-4 and SS-5, which dated back to the early 1960s. Unlike the SS-4 and SS-5, the SS-20 was mobile and had a range of 3,000 miles (4,828 km). It was launched from specially designed military trucks. The SS-20 was more accurate and reliable than the missiles it replaced. The SS-20 was also equipped with three MIRV warheads.

Each warhead could create an explosion equal to 250,000 tons of TNT. In the western part of the Soviet Union, the SS-20s were aimed at Europe. In the east, China was the target.

In 1987 the Soviet Union agreed to dismantle all of its SS-20s as part of the Intermediate-range Nuclear Force (INF) treaty with the United States. A large section of an SS-20 is on display at the Smithsonian Institution's Air and Space Museum in Washington, D.C.

Protesting the New Missiles

The West German and British governments agreed to accept the new U.S. missiles in their territories. But some citizens in these countries, and in other NATO states, did not want the Pershings and cruise missiles. Hundreds of thousands of West

Germans marched to protest the arrival of the new missiles. Said one protester, "What was always dangerous was that Germany would be the nuclear battlefield. That made the people very upset and angry." In England a group of women tried to keep missiles out of the Greenham Common air base. At one point several thousand people joined that protest.

The Soviet Union also protested the arrival of the new missiles. Soviet leaders feared that the Pershings could be used to launch offensive strikes against targets within their country. They did not see the Pershings as a response to their introduction of the SS-20. To Brezhnev and other Soviet leaders, the Pershings were a new step forward in the arms race.

In June 1978 Soviet leaders met to discuss the new threats to détente. Brezhnev said:

> A serious deterioration...of the situation has occurred. And the primary source of this deterioration is the growing aggression of the foreign policy of the Carter government, the continually more sharply anti-Soviet statements of the President himself and of his closest colleagues—[for example,] those of Brzezinski. Carter is...intent upon struggling for his election to a new term as President of the USA under the banner of anti-Soviet policy and a return to the "cold war."

As the two sides argued about their missiles, the Soviet Union stepped up its campaign against its dissidents. The conviction of Anatoly Shcharansky for treason in July 1978 sparked outrage in America. The U.S. government canceled some trade agreements, and trips by American officials to the Soviet Union were called off.

Relations also soured over America's growing ties with China and events in Africa. Carter established official relations with the Communist Chinese on January 1, 1979. The Soviet leaders feared that the Americans would aid the Chinese at the expense of the Soviet Union. In Africa the United States and the Soviet Union had opposing interests in a region called the "Horn of Africa." Fighting

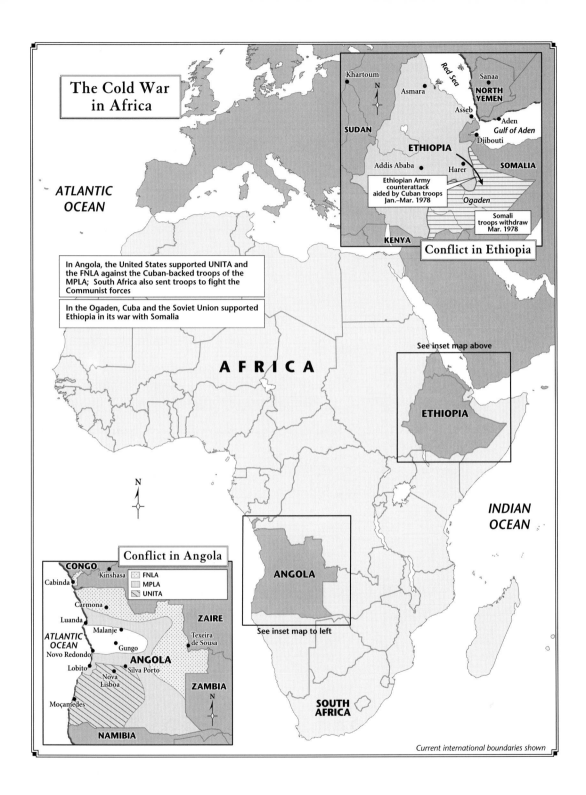

The Cold War in Africa

ATLANTIC OCEAN

N

Conflict in Ethiopia

Khartoum

SUDAN

N

Asmara

Red Sea

Sanaa

NORTH YEMEN

Asseb

Aden

Gulf of Aden

Djibouti

ETHIOPIA

Addis Ababa

Harer

SOMALIA

Ethiopian Army counterattack aided by Cuban troops Jan.–Mar. 1978

Ogaden

Somali troops withdraw Mar. 1978

KENYA

In Angola, the United States supported UNITA and the FNLA against the Cuban-backed troops of the MPLA; South Africa also sent troops to fight the Communist forces

In the Ogaden, Cuba and the Soviet Union supported Ethiopia in its war with Somalia

A F R I C A

See inset map above

ETHIOPIA

N

INDIAN OCEAN

Conflict in Angola

FNLA
MPLA
UNITA

CONGO

Cabinda

Kinshasa

Carmona

Luanda

Malanje

ZAIRE

Texeira de Sousa

ATLANTIC OCEAN

Gungo

Novo Redondo

ANGOLA

Silva Porto

Lobito

Nova Lisboa

Moçamedes

ZAMBIA

N

NAMIBIA

ANGOLA

See inset map to left

SOUTH AFRICA

Current international boundaries shown

had erupted there in 1977, and the Soviet Union continued to have influence. Said Brzezinski, "The Horn of Africa was not important to America...of itself, but it was important as a measure...of how the Soviets were interpreting détente."

Places ▸ THE HORN OF AFRICA

The Horn of Africa refers to the part of eastern Africa that juts out into the Indian Ocean, near the Gulf of Aden. It includes the countries of Ethiopia, Somalia, and Djibouti. For many years

Somali troops on horseback

Ethiopia had close ties to the West. But during the 1970s, socialists led by Colonel Mengistu Haile Mariam took control of the government. In 1977 they formed military relations with the Soviet Union, receiving military advisors and large quantities of arms.

Until then, the Soviet Union had been friendly with the Somalian government of Mohammed Siad Barre. Somalia and Ethiopia had been traditional foes. As Ethiopia moved closer to Moscow, Barre turned to the West for support. Barre wanted to take control of a region in Ethiopia called the Ogaden. President Carter, however, refused to support Somalia in a war against Ethiopia. Barre attacked anyway, and the Soviet Union and Cuba quickly sent troops and weapons to Mengistu. With this help Ethiopia repelled the Somalian invasion. To the Americans the Soviet involvement was a bad sign—it seemed that the Soviet Union was trying to take a more active military role in African affairs.

The Rise and Fall of SALT II

Despite the problems between their countries, Carter and Brezhnev moved forward with talks to limit nuclear weapons. In June 1979 the two leaders met in Vienna, Austria, for their first and only summit meeting. Carter hoped he and Brezhnev could discuss a wide range of issues, but Brezhnev was ill and not prepared for lengthy discussions. Their only major accomplishment was signing the SALT II treaty.

The treaty was basically the same agreement Brezhnev and Ford had approved five years earlier in Vladivostok. SALT II limited each side to 2,400 strategic nuclear delivery vehicles—various types of missiles. This number would be cut to 2,250 in 1982. Each country had tried to limit new weapons on the other side. Once again the Americans wanted to include the Backfire bomber. The Soviet Union hoped to limit a new experimental U.S. missile, the MX. Neither side got what it wanted.

SALT II was important for Soviet leaders. They hoped to limit weapons production eventually, because the arms race was becoming too costly. Soviet general Nikolai Denitov said, "Our expenditure on all weapons had begun to have a negative effect. It was affecting the growth of production. It was affecting the living standards of the population."

Carter and his advisors saw SALT II as a positive step in reducing arms. But to some Americans, the treaty and the general U.S. policy of détente gave the Soviet Union too much power. Paul Nitze had advised U.S. presidents on foreign affairs since the 1940s. He opposed SALT II, saying, "The United States is being pushed around in the world.... [I]t is time for the United States to stand up and not be a patsy." The treaty needed approval by the U.S. Senate, but some leading senators, including Henry Jackson, opposed it. SALT II was never ratified by the Senate.

The fate of SALT II was sealed in December 1979. The Soviet Union launched an invasion against neighboring Afghanistan. This was the first direct Soviet military campaign since the invasion of Czechoslovakia in 1968. The era of détente was over.

5

TROUBLE
ON TWO
CONTINENTS

During the 1970s both the United States and the Soviet Union had a growing interest in Afghanistan. This Muslim country bordered the southern part of the Soviet Union. Russia, under its old *czarist* government, had tried to influence events in this neighboring land. The Soviet Communists continued that policy. Afghanistan was also close to the Persian Gulf and the oil-rich countries of the Middle East. The gulf was an important route for oil going to the West and Japan. The United States worried about any developments in that region that might threaten the supply of oil. Afghanistan became another hot spot in the Cold War.

A Reluctant Invasion

In April 1978 pro-Soviet *Marxist* leaders took over the government of Afghanistan. This takeover came after the previous leader had moved closer to the West and broken off relations with the Soviet Union. The new Afghan leaders had been trained by Moscow and received Soviet backing for the government takeover. These Afghans were socialists, and they asked the Soviet Union to help them create a socialist society. However, the changes upset many Afghans who were Muslims, followers of the Islamic religion. The most devoted followers of Islam are called *fundamentalists*. They formed small armies and began attacking government forces. The fundamentalists called themselves *mujahedeen*—"soldiers of god."

In 1979 President Jimmy Carter sent some basic aid—communications equipment—to the mujahedeen. By this time the Afghan government had already asked the Soviet Union to send in troops to help fight the Muslim rebels. At first Soviet leaders refused. Said Soviet premier Aleksei Kosygin, "The negative factors would be enormous. Most countries would immediately go against us." For the time being, the Soviet Union sent only military equipment, not soldiers.

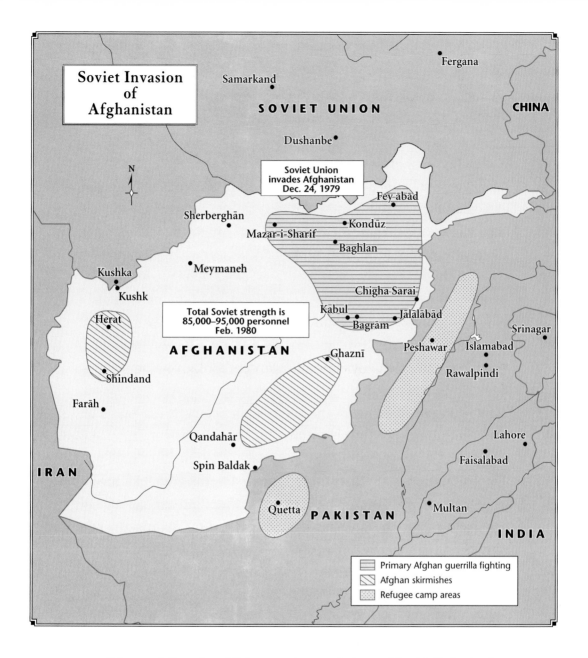

Soviet Invasion of Afghanistan

Fergana

Samarkand

SOVIET UNION

CHINA

Dushanbe

Soviet Union
invades Afghanistan
Dec. 24, 1979

Fey-abad

Sherberghān

Kondūz

Mazar-i-Sharif

Baghlan

Kushka

Meymaneh

Kushk

Total Soviet strength is
85,000–95,000 personnel
Feb. 1980

Chigha Sarai

Kabul

Jalalabad

Herat

Bagrām

Srinagar

AFGHANISTAN

Ghaznī

Peshawar

Islamabad

Shindand

Rawalpindi

Farāh

Qandahār

Lahore

Spin Baldak

Faisalabad

IRAN

Quetta

PAKISTAN

Multan

INDIA

	Primary Afghan guerrilla fighting
	Afghan skirmishes
	Refugee camp areas

Meanwhile, the Afghan prime minister, Hazifullah Amin, pushed for his own socialist reforms. Soviet leaders thought that he was moving too quickly with these changes. Amin also arrested and executed his government's political opponents, many of whom were Muslims. This angered the fundamentalists. The United States debated sending more aid to the mujahedeen. Brzezinski said yes; Secretary of State Vance was reluctant. Instead, the Americans encouraged Pakistan to arm and train the rebels.

While the fighting went on, the Soviet Union made plans to get rid of Amin and slow the reforms. Amin learned of these plans. He had his chief political rival—Nur Mohammad Taraki—killed, and seemed ready to consider closer ties to the West. The Soviet *Politburo*—the ruling body of the Communist party—debated invading Afghanistan. Some military leaders had warned that Afghanistan would be "Russia's Vietnam." Once in the country, Soviet troops might find it impossible to win a military victory. Karen Brutents, a member of the Soviet Communist party, recalled, "I said that military intervention in Afghanistan would be very difficult for our army.... One only has to consider the conditions in Afghanistan, its geography, its history, and especially the independent nature of the Afghans." But others, such as KGB General Vladimir Kryuchkov, believed "that if we didn't go into Afghanistan then some other countries would. The intervention of these states could destabilize the situation on the Soviet-Afghan border and in the region as a whole."

In December 1979 Soviet leaders finally decided it was time to invade. The arms race seemed to be speeding up again, and détente was already in decline; the Soviet Union had nothing to lose. On December 24 Soviet troops and tanks moved across the border into Afghanistan. It was the first Soviet invasion of a country outside the Warsaw Pact. Within two days special Soviet forces had assassinated Amin and put a new leader into power.

Places   AFGHANISTAN

The mountainous country of Afghanistan has been called the crossroads of East and West. An Islamic country, Afghanistan sits on the southern border of the former Soviet republics of Turkmenistan, Uzbekistan, and Tajikistan. The country is also wedged between Iran to the west and Pakistan to the east and south. One small part of Afghanistan borders China. The capital city of Kabul sits near the Hindu Kush mountains, which reach a height of 25,000 feet (7,620 m). A famous route through the mountains, the Khyber Pass, links Afghanistan with Pakistan.

For centuries various foreign powers invaded Afghanistan and tried to rule it. Great Britain controlled most of Afghanistan from the late 19th century through 1919. That year British and Afghan forces waged their third and last war against each other. The Afghans won the war and their country's full independence. A king ruled Afghanistan until 1964, when a constitutional monarchy, providing for the election of representatives, was introduced. This is the same kind of government system used in Great Britain.

After the Soviet invasion of Afghanistan, Soviet troops remained in the country for nine years. When the

Soviet tanks begin the 1979 invasion of Afghanistan.

Soviets finally withdrew, Afghanistan remained a war zone as different groups within the country struggled for power. During the mid-1990s, the *Taliban*, a group of Islamic fundamentalists, won control of most of the country. They fought with U.S. weapons originally sent to help the mujahedeen battle Soviet forces. The Taliban used the Islamic holy book, the *Koran*, as the supposed source of their laws. They faced continued resistance from Afghans who wanted a more democratic government.

Sources   SOVIET REACTION TO THE AFGHAN SITUATION

Throughout 1979 the Soviet government faced a rapidly changing situation in Afghanistan. The first selection below comes from an October 4 conversation between Leonid Brezhnev and East German leader Erich Honecker.

We have given Afghanistan more than a little economic support...and have supplied them with significant amounts of weapons and military equipment....

Frankly, we are not pleased by all of Amin's methods and actions. He is very power-driven. In the past he repeatedly revealed disproportionate harshness. But with regard to his basic political platform, he has decidedly confirmed to the course of...furthering cooperation with the Soviet Union and other countries of the Socialist community....

...[W]e will continue to support Afghanistan and give it a variety of support and help in its fight against foreign aggression and the domestic counterrevolution.

This second selection is from a personal memorandum sent to Brezhnev in December by Yuri Andropov, head of the KGB.

After...September of this year, the situation in Afghanistan began to undertake an undesirable turn for us....

...[A]larming information started to arrive about Amin's secret activities, forewarning of a possible political shift to the West.... All this has created...the danger of losing the gains made by the April [1978] revolution.... [There has been] a growth of anti-Soviet sentiment within the population....

We have two battalions stationed in Kabul.... It appears that this is entirely sufficient for a successful operation.... The implementation of the given operation would allow us to decide the question of defending the gains of the April revolution...and securing our position in this country.

The Americans Respond

Carter reacted angrily to the invasion. He called Brezhnev on the *Hot Line*, the direct communications link between American and Soviet leaders. Carter said that the Soviet move was a "clear threat" to peace. Brzezinski saw the invasion as another major crisis in a part of the world that was already unstable. In Iran, Americans were being held hostage by Islamic fundamentalists. The country—once a U.S. ally—was now a bitter foe. U.S. relations with Pakistan were shaky, and the government there did not seem strong. The region also bordered the critical oil supplies of the Middle East. Brzezinski feared that the Soviet Union might move from Afghanistan into neighboring countries. In a memorandum to Carter, he warned, "If the Soviets succeed in Afghanistan...the age-long dream of Moscow to have direct access to the Indian Ocean will have been fulfilled."

On January 23, 1980, Carter gave his State of the Union speech. He said, "The implications of the Soviet invasion of Afghanistan could pose the most serious threat to the peace since the Second World War." Soon after, he initiated diplomatic and military responses to the invasion. The U.S. government canceled planned grain and technology sales to the Soviet Union. It also disclosed its intention to sell weapons for the first time to China. In the UN, America led the effort to condemn the invasion. Carter also revealed plans for new U.S. naval bases in eastern Africa and the Middle East. He increased the defense budget and won congressional approval for mandatory registration for a possible *military draft*. The thinking was that if the country went to war, the government would be prepared to draft new soldiers. Carter also withdrew his support for the SALT II treaty.

Further, the United States increased its aid to the mujahedeen. Most of this was sent through Pakistan. The CIA also gave weapons to the rebels. Some of these arms were made by the Soviet Union and bought from other countries. "And at some point," Brzezinski later said, "we started buying arms...from the Soviet army in Afghanistan, because that army was increasingly corrupt."

Brezhnev rejected the U.S. criticisms of the invasion. He said that the Soviet Union had been invited into Afghanistan. During 1980 the Soviet Union increased its forces there to roughly 90,000. They guarded

One of the mujahedeen waits for battle.

cities, major roads, and airports, while the Afghan army fought the mujahedeen. Soviet soldiers were told that American troops were fighting there, too. Said one Soviet soldier, "After we took our first Afghan prisoners, we started to realize that the Americans were not there.... But the KGB officers said, 'Oh, they're in the rear.'... But the more operations we carried out, the more we realized that the Americans were not there."

The Soviet troops were drawn deeper into the conflict. They won battles, but the rebels continued to fight, withdrawing afterward to hide in the mountains. Meanwhile, events in Poland began to draw Soviet and American attention away from Afghanistan.

Culture — COLD WAR SPORTS

To protest the Soviet invasion of Afghanistan, President Carter decided that U.S. athletes should not attend the 1980 Summer Olympics, which were being held in Moscow. He tried to get other countries to go along with the boycott. About 60 countries eventually boycotted the games, but some major U.S. allies, including Great Britain and France, did send athletes to Moscow. Four years later the Soviet Union organized a much smaller boycott of the Summer Games held in Los Angeles.

The 1980 Olympic Games were not the first ones affected by Cold War politics. East Germany was not allowed to send a team to the 1952 games in Helsinki. Only athletes from West Germany represented Germany that year. In 1956 a water polo match between the Soviet Union and Hungary turned violent, reflecting increased Hungarian unrest over Soviet control of their country. Communist China boycotted the Olympics from 1956 to 1980 because the International Olympic Committee allowed Taiwan to compete. The Communists claimed that Taiwan was merely a province of China, not the seat of the legitimate government of the entire nation. The conflicts in the Middle East spilled over into the 1972 games in Munich, Germany. Palestinian terrorists kidnapped members of the Israeli team and murdered two of them. Nine more were killed in a rescue attempt.

Athletic competition at the games sometimes mirrored the Cold War competition between the East and West. To the Communists, winning more gold medals than the Americans supposedly showed that their system was better than the capitalist system. Soviet and Eastern European coaches routinely gave their athletes steroids and other illegal drugs to improve their performances in an effort to win more medals. Americans never went that far, but some believed that U.S. victories over the Soviet athletes were extremely important. Some games took on a larger political importance.

One such clash came in 1972 on the basketball court in Munich. The Americans had won the gold medal in basketball in seven consecutive Olympics. A controversial call at the end of the gold medal game in Munich gave the Soviet Union a 51–50 win over the United States. Another historic upset came at the 1980 Winter Games in Lake Placid, New York. Just as the Americans dominated basketball, the Soviet Union dominated ice hockey. But that year the U.S. team beat the Soviet squad and went on to win the gold medal. The victory was both an athletic and a patriotic triumph.

Polish Troubles

After the 1968 Soviet invasion of Czechoslovakia, most of Eastern Europe remained calm and firmly under Soviet control. Poland, however, was an exception. In 1970 and 1976, Polish workers protested rising prices of basic goods. The protests turned into violent demonstrations. The workers

Karol Wojtyla, better known as Pope John Paul II

and Polish intellectuals began acting together against the government. One of the protesters in both 1970 and 1976 was Lech Walesa. An electrician, Walesa worked at the Lenin Shipyards in Gdansk. He emerged as a leader of the movement to end communism in Poland.

Events outside Poland also influenced the growing desire to topple communism there. In 1978 Karol Wojtyla, a Pole, became Pope John Paul II. As pope he was the leader of the Roman Catholic Church. For centuries Poland had been a largely Roman Catholic nation. Under the Communists Poland did not have any officially approved religions. The government tried to limit the influence and activities of the Catholic Church. But most Poles still considered themselves Catholics. The Catholic Church was associated with Polish nationalism, a desire for Poles to throw off Soviet-influenced rule and have their own independent nation. John Paul, the first Polish pope ever, gave many Poles new inspiration.

In 1979 John Paul returned to his homeland. When he spoke in Warsaw, 250,000 people came to hear him. Said Walesa, "[T]he Pope's visit in 1979 was like a gift from God. It fit ideally with our fight against this terrible communist system, based on lies, falsehoods and manipulations. This gift of God let us...regain the trust in the basic values: the power of truth, the power of freedom."

People   LECH WALESA

"The Polish nation," said Lech Walesa, "has the ability to fight, lose, and still not be conquered." The Polish people were unable to end Communist rule in Poland in the 1970s and early 1980s, but Walesa helped the Poles eventually win their freedom.

Walesa was born on September 29, 1943, in Popowo, Poland. He began working at the Lenin Shipyards in Gdansk in 1967. Three years later he led protests at the shipyards after the government ordered increases in food prices. The protests also reflected a general hatred of the Communist regime. Walesa came to realize that violence would not end communism in Poland. Instead, he and others decided to form workers' unions to challenge the government. His activities as a dissident led to several arrests between 1976 and 1980.

In 1980 Walesa was out of work when protests began again at the Lenin Shipyards. He climbed the yard's fence and joined the workers, who immediately named him their leader. As strikes spread throughout Poland, Walesa met with the government and worked out a plan to allow unions for the workers. This workers' movement was called Solidarity, and Walesa was its leader. He became an internationally known figure.

Solidarity did not last—the Polish government declared martial law the following year and outlawed the workers' union. Walesa, as a leading dissident, was often arrested and kept under close government watch. When he won the Nobel Peace Prize in 1983, he was unable to leave Poland to collect his prize. He feared that if he left, the government would not let him return.

At the end of the 1980s, as communism came to an end in Poland, Walesa spoke out for reforms. In 1990 he was elected president of Poland, and he held that office until 1995. After his presidency, he remained active in Polish politics.

The Rise of Solidarity

In July 1980 the Polish government announced another huge increase in food prices. In protest, workers began an illegal strike. The 17,000 workers at the Lenin Shipyards in Gdansk joined the strike in August. Walesa led the strike at the shipyards, and he became head of a committee that linked all the striking factories. This commit-

Workers line a fence at Gdansk's Lenin Shipyards during the July 1980 strike.

tee soon became known as *Solidarnosc*, Polish for "Solidarity." The leaders of Solidarity met with the government and demanded the legal right to form an independent union and go on strike. They also asked for greater religious freedom and a free press. The

Solidarity leader Lech Walesa waves to supporters.

government gave in to most of their demands.

The Polish people celebrated Solidarity's success. Said one Solidarity member, "For the first time they had a taste of being citizens with civil liberties, which you don't forget. For someone who had lived under communism it was like...fresh air. It was like having your identity for the first time."

Walesa and Solidarity received major news coverage in the West. President Carter welcomed the changes in Poland. He praised the Poles, saying they had "set an example for all those who cherish freedom and human dignity." U.S. trade groups sent aid to Solidarity, such as printing presses and radio equipment.

The Soviet Union was not pleased with Solidarity's growing power. In December 1980, Warsaw Pact troops massed around Poland's borders. The CIA warned Carter that the Soviet Union and its allies might invade Poland. Soviet troops had been preparing since August to enter Poland and help Polish leaders introduce military rule. When the leaders warned that the presence of foreign troops would make matters worse, the Soviet Union decided to wait.

The man given the job of crushing Solidarity was General Wojciech Jaruzelski. In October 1981 he took over as head of the Polish Communist party. By then Solidarity had almost ten million members. It was more than a labor movement; it was a political force challenging the authority of the Communist party. In December, Solidarity proposed holding a national vote on whether the country should have a non-Communist government. Strikes were still going on around Poland, and food supplies were low. Given these conditions, and under pressure from the Soviet Union, Jaruzelski took action.

On December 13 the general declared martial law in Poland. This put the military in charge of the country and many key industries. Jaruzelski also banned public meetings and arrested leaders of Solidarity, including Walesa. Poland was cut off from the outside world. Jaruzelski told the Poles, "Heavy is the responsibility which I bear at this dramatic moment of Polish history. It is my duty to take responsibility. Poland's future is at stake."

In the United States, Ronald Reagan was now president. He cut off most economic ties with Poland and threatened further action "if this repression continues." Reagan had campaigned for president as a devoted anti-Communist. To him the events in Poland and Afghanistan confirmed that détente was a failure. He played down détente in favor of fiercer competition. The United States, he believed, had to beat the Soviet Union in the Cold War.

People   WOJCIECH JARUZELSKI

During the Polish crisis of 1981, General Wojciech Jaruzelski, with his tinted glasses, became a well-known figure in the West. By the end of 1981, Jaruzelski held three key positions in the Polish government: defense minister, prime minister, and leader of the Communist party. He promised the Soviet Union that he would take a hard line with Solidarity, and he stuck to his word.

Jaruzelski was born on July 6, 1923, in Kurow, Poland. At the start of World War I, he and his family were captured by the Soviet army and sent to the Soviet Union. Jaruzelski was forced to work in coal mines until the Soviet government selected him to receive military training. He joined the Polish First Army, a Soviet-backed force, and took part in the liberation of Warsaw in 1945. After the war he fought against the Polish Homeland Army, which opposed Communist rule in Poland.

Jaruzelski joined the Communist party in 1947 and rose through the ranks of the army. In 1968 he was named minister of defense. During the 1970 demonstrations, Jaruzelski transmitted the orders from the Communist leadership to open fire on the protesters.

Jaruzelski became Poland's prime minister in February 1981. Eight months later he was also named first secretary of the Communist party. After the crackdown on December 13, martial law was in place for 18 months. Poland continued to suffer economically, and Solidarity remained influential. Jaruzelski resigned as prime minister in 1985 but remained in charge of the Communist party. In 1989 Communist leaders held talks with Solidarity about reforming the Polish government. Under an agreement with the labor union, Jaruzelski was allowed to remain in the government as president. Jaruzelski resigned in late 1990 and Lech Walesa was elected president. In later years Jaruzelski faced criminal charges for his role in the 1970 government attack on protesters.

After December 13, 1981, armored vehicles such as this one enforced martial law in Poland.

RETURN
OF THE
COLD
WARRIORS

During the 1970s Ronald Reagan emerged as a leading spokesman for the right wing, or the *conservatives*, of the Republican party. The conservatives favored reducing taxes and government spending on some social programs. They wanted to end laws that restricted how companies conducted their business. In foreign policy they sought to build up the U.S. military and challenge the Soviet Union.

At Vienna in June 1979, Carter and Brezhnev signed the SALT II accords.

When President Carter was working on SALT II, Reagan attacked the treaty. He said, "[I]sn't it time that we made [Carter] understand we don't really care whether [the Russians] like us or not[?] We want to be respected."

During the 1980 presidential campaign, Carter proudly noted his foreign policy successes. He had helped Israel and Egypt sign a peace treaty, and the United States had created official diplomatic ties with China. The U.S. had also improved its relations with some African countries. Finally U.S. defense spending was on the rise, with new weapons being introduced. But Reagan, running as the Republican nominee for the presidency, believed Carter had not done enough, especially in limiting Moscow's gains. Reagan argued that the Soviet Union "underlies all the unrest that is going on. If they weren't engaged in this game of dominoes, there wouldn't be any hot spots in the world."

Reagan's conservative message appealed to many American voters. And Carter's problems, particularly the sputtering U.S. economy and the Iranian hostage crisis, had made him unpopular. In November 1980 Reagan easily beat Carter for the U.S. presidency. The conservatives were now in control in Washington. Relations between the United States and the Soviet Union were about to become even more confrontational.

RONALD REAGAN

When Ronald Reagan became president of the United States, he promised to put the Soviet Union on the "ash heap of history." Reagan was sometimes criticized by some Americans and Western allies for his tough talk. But his policies helped force the Soviet Union to halt the arms race and lead the way to the end of the Cold War.

Reagan was born on February 6, 1911, in Tampico, Illinois. After a brief career in sports broadcasting, Reagan went to Hollywood and became a movie actor. During his career he appeared in more than 50 films. After World War II, Reagan served as president of the Screen Actors Guild, a labor union for movie actors. He spoke out against the influence of Communists in Hollywood. Reagan gradually became interested in politics and entered his first race in 1966. Running as a conservative Republican, he was elected governor of California.

Reagan ran for the Republican presidential nomination in 1976 but lost to President Gerald Ford. In the 1980 election, Reagan won his party's nomination, and he beat Jimmy Carter for the presidency. Reagan's warm personality and conservative views helped him win reelection easily in 1984.

To his political foes, Reagan was just an actor who did not understand the complexities of the world. But Reagan had a clear sense of what he wanted to do, and he restored the American people's confidence in their country. Reagan was also willing to work for arms reduction with the Soviet Union once he thought the United States could deal from a position of strength. Reagan drew sharp criticism for the Iran-Contra affair, which involved the illegal sale of arms to Iran. Reagan was particularly attacked for not keeping track of what his aides did. But overall, most Americans respected his leadership and his handling of the Cold War.

Arming the U.S. and Its Friends

While still running for president, Reagan had said about the arms race, "[T]here's one going on right now, but there's only one side racing." To Reagan and other conservatives, Carter had not done enough to keep the U.S. military strong. Soon after taking office, Reagan proposed a huge increase in defense spending—more than $32 billion. The money was to go for such items as new ships, new long-range bombers, new nuclear weapons called *neutron bombs*, and improved conventional forces. At the same time, Reagan made one move that the Soviet government welcomed: He allowed U.S. farmers to again sell grain to the Soviet Union. Reagan did this for the benefit of the farmers, not the Soviet Union.

Reagan's key advisors included Secretary of Defense Caspar Weinberger and Secretary of State Alexander Haig. Both were convinced that the United States had to be ready for war against the Soviet Union or its allies. "I had no doubt," Weinberger said, "that the Soviet goal was world domination." Soviet troops were still involved in Afghanistan, so Reagan increased aid to the mujahedeen. Reagan and his advisors also saw a Soviet threat closer to home, in Latin America. Nicaragua and El Salvador were the new focus of America's Cold War policy.

In Nicaragua a Marxist government led by a group called the Sandinistas seized power in 1979. The Sandinistas ended the corrupt rule of Anastasio Somoza, whose family had controlled Nicaragua for more than 40 years. The Somozas were strong anti-Communists and friendly with the United States. The American government—and many Nicaraguans—opposed the new Marxist government. Sandinista leader Daniel Ortega turned to the Soviet Union and Cuba for aid. The Soviet Union sent weapons, and the Cubans sent advisors. Under Reagan the United States started sending money and military aid to the Contras, Nicaraguans who opposed the Sandinistas.

Nicaraguan Contras train for a war against their country's Marxist, pro-Soviet government.

In El Salvador another group of Marxist rebels was trying to take power from a pro-American government. Although the government had been elected democratically, the Salvadoran military sometimes used force, in the form of so-called death squads, to silence the government's critics, including Roman Catholic priests and nuns. Late in 1980 three American nuns were assassinated by the Salvadoran National Guard. Still, the U.S. government continued to help the Salvadoran government against the rebels. The Americans wanted to prevent further Soviet and Cuban gains in Central America. Early in 1981 Haig said, "What we're watching is a four-phased operation. Phase one has been completed—the seizure of Nicaragua. Next is El Salvador, to be followed by Honduras and Guatemala.... I would call it a priority target list—a hit list if you will—for the ultimate takeover of Central America."

Military and financial aid for the Contras and the Salvadoran government kept increasing. Congress tried to end the U.S. funding for the Contras. It passed laws in 1983 and 1984 to cut off aid to the Contras unless Congress approved it first. Reagan's advisors got around these laws by secretly passing military aid to the Contras. Some of the money for this aid came from illegal arms sales to Iran. Officially the United States and Iran still had no ties because of the earlier hostage crisis and Iran's ongoing support of terrorism in the Middle East. This so-called Iran-Contra affair became public in 1986, leading to legal investigations of the U.S. government's actions. Reagan claimed that he did not know about the illegal dealings.

A young Nicaraguan shows his support for the Sandinistas.

Places — NICARAGUA

Nicaragua lies across the middle of Central America, between the Caribbean Sea and the Pacific Ocean. Its neighbors are Honduras to the north and Costa Rica to the south. Its capital is Managua.

Nicaragua was controlled by Spain from the mid-16th century until 1821. Some Americans took an interest in the country soon after, as they hoped to limit British influence in Central America and expand the presence of the United States. During the last decades of the 19th century, the U.S. government considered building a canal through Nicaragua to link the Pacific Ocean and the Caribbean Sea. The United States later built a canal in nearby Panama, and it began exercising even greater control over the region. Beginning in 1909 the United States sent marines into Nicaragua three times to secure pro-U.S. governments. The final military occupation lasted from 1925 until 1933.

A Nicaraguan named Cesar Sandino led fighting against the U.S. troops in an attempt to win Nicaraguan freedom from U.S. control. The Sandinista movement of the 1980s was named for him.

The Somoza family took power in Nicaragua in 1936 and ruled until the Sandinistas took power in 1979. The U.S. policy of arming the Contras against the Sandinistas helped fuel a bloody civil war that lasted until 1989. In democratic elections the next year, Sandinista leader Daniel Ortega lost his bid to become Nicaragua's president. The position went to Violeta Chamorra, who favored good ties with the United States. Ortega lost another race for the presidency in 1996.

The Bomb KILL THE PEOPLE, SAVE THE BUILDINGS

The neutron bomb was a controversial weapon during the first years of the Reagan administration. The first of these bombs was created in 1974, but President Carter decided not to deploy it. Reagan reversed that decision—he wanted to stock neutron warheads for possible use in Europe. In the early 1980s, protesters in some Western European countries demonstrated against the neutron bomb.

A neutron bomb is also known as an enhanced radiation (ER) weapon. Neutrons are highly radioactive particles. Unlike other nuclear weapons, the neutron bomb relies on a high dose of radiation from neutrons, rather than the blast from its explosion, to kill the enemy. It was designed for battlefield use. The neutron bomb was referred to as a "landlord bomb," since it would kill people but supposedly do minimal damage to any nearby buildings.

The United States built three types of neutron bombs. The last was retired from service in 1992. It is believed that some countries still have neutron bombs in their nuclear weapon arsenals.

Continuing Talks of Peace

Although Reagan pursued the Cold War with vigor, diplomacy was practiced, as well. The Soviet Union entered talks with representatives from the UN about ending the fighting in Afghanistan. Soviet leaders said that they would pull out their troops, but they wanted to make sure a pro-Soviet government was set up in Afghanistan. The United States did not believe the Soviet army would leave peacefully. Also, it served U.S. interests for the Soviet Union to be bogged down in a long war. The negotiations went nowhere.

The United States and the Soviet Union also began new talks on reducing nuclear weapons. Reagan called these *Strategic Arms Reduction Talks* (START) and proposed huge cuts. However, the first proposal was for a reduction in the weapons that the Soviet Union relied on most, so Moscow refused to go along.

As President Reagan went ahead with plans to introduce Pershing II missiles in Europe, protesters in the United States and Western Europe took to the streets. In June 1982 an estimated 500,000 people marched in New York City and then held a rally in Central Park. Some doctors and religious leaders in the United States began to speak out against the renewed arms race. George Kennan, one of the early shapers of U.S. Cold War strategy, had already joined the debate. His message was simple: "Cease this madness."

In November 1982 the leadership in the Soviet Union changed. After many years of frail health, Leonid Brezhnev died. His successor was Yuri Andropov. He called for new cuts in U.S. nuclear weapons and suggested removing them altogether from some parts of Europe. But Andropov refused to accept limits on Soviet SS-20 missiles.

Although a strong supporter of the Cold War, Andropov felt some pressure to consider arms reductions. The Soviet Union was finding it difficult to pay for an arms race, fight in Afghanistan, and support its allies. Soviet citizens were already suffering. Said one Moscow resident, "The standard of living was very low. We lived from pay day to pay day. We couldn't feed our children properly.... We used to spend three, four, five hours [waiting in lines] for some lousy sausage!"

But Reagan was not ready to ease up U.S. pressure. He saw the Soviet Union as an "evil empire." And he was preparing to announce a new element to the arms race. He called it the *Strategic Defense Initiative* (SDI), but most people knew it as "Star Wars."

People ☆ YURI ANDROPOV

Before taking over as head of the Soviet Communist party, Yuri Andropov was head of the KGB. In that position, he led a vicious campaign against Soviet dissidents. He believed in strong Communist party rule and pursuing the Cold War with vigor.

Andropov was born on June 15, 1914, in Ngutskaya, Russia. At 16 he joined the Communist youth league (Komsomol) and earned important positions in the organization. After World War II, Andropov served briefly in Moscow, and then he was sent to Hungary. He was the Soviet ambassador there during the Hungarian Uprising of 1956. Andropov did his best to convince Moscow that an invasion was essential to end the uprising.

Andropov returned to the Soviet Union in 1957 and continued working for the Communist party. In 1967 he was appointed head of the KGB. During Andropov's service at the agency, the KGB carried out new, more violent programs to silence Soviet dissidents.

In November 1982, days after the death of Leonid Brezhnev, Andropov was named the general secretary of the Communist party, making him the leader of the Soviet Union. Two of his supposed goals were to end corruption in the Soviet government and improve the economy. He was unsuccessful in both efforts. After just 15 months in power, Andropov died of liver failure on February 9, 1984.

Star Wars

Segment
#6
Star Wars

President Reagan was uncomfortable with the old nuclear strategy of mutual assured destruction. Under MAD both the Soviet Union and the United States had enough ICBMs to destroy the other side many times over. According to Donald Regan, a Reagan aide, the president believed "these types of weapons needed some kind of defense. What is the defense against an intercontinental ballistic missile? It has to be some kind of shield. Star Wars was to be that shield."

Reagan proposed creating a defense system that could shoot down airborne Soviet missiles before they reached the ground. In a speech on March 23, 1983, he said,

> *I know this is a formidable technical task, one that may not be accomplished before the end of this century. I call upon the scientific community in our country, those who gave us nuclear weapons, to turn their great talents now to the cause of mankind and world peace—to give us the means of rendering these nuclear weapons impotent and obsolete.*

The idea of Star Wars stunned Soviet leaders, who feared that the arms race would now increasingly move into space. The defense system, it was claimed, would also upset the nuclear balance. The United States supposedly might feel confident about launching a surprise attack, since its defense system could potentially destroy any Soviet missiles fired in response. Andropov saw the move as an unwelcome challenge. He said, "All attempts at achieving military superiority over the Soviet Union are futile. The Soviet Union will never let that happen."

Star Wars also troubled some of America's European allies and U.S. citizens. The defensive shield would cover only the United States. The Soviet Union could still launch successful nuclear attacks on Europe. British prime minister Margaret Thatcher was usually a strong supporter of President Reagan, but she opposed Star Wars when it was first introduced. American critics said the plan would cost too much money. Most important of all, the plan was technically impossible. There was no way a defense system could stop an overwhelming Soviet missile attack. Still, Reagan pushed ahead with SDI.

Technology — LASERS IN SPACE

In the first years of Star Wars development, Ronald Reagan and the scientists with whom he consulted thought about placing lasers in space. *Laser* stands for "Light Amplification by Stimulated Emission of Radiation." Lasers are highly focused beams of light made up of just one color. The waves in a regular beam of light have many colors and tend to scatter. A laser beam can be focused down to a tiny point and can have the power to cut through a diamond. A powerful laser can also shoot down a missile.

The early research for Star Wars moved slowly. At one point the military altered some test results to make the system appear better than it was. Today, work on laser weapons continues, with somewhat better results. However, these weapons are not meant to be placed in space.

Some of the lasers being tested are designed to be used on the battlefield. The U.S. Army is working on lasers that can shoot down incoming artillery shells. The U.S. Air Force is testing an airborne laser that would be carried on a plane. This laser would be able to shoot down longer-range missiles. Planes carrying such lasers would fly near enemy territory and fire at missiles soon after they were launched.

Lasers have some distinct advantages over conventional weapons. Laser beams travel at the speed of light, so their paths can be corrected almost immediately if they are off target. They are also cheaper to use than missiles designed to intercept other missiles. But some critics of laser weapons say they are still too expensive and have not been proven to work in battle.

As President Reagan talked about the "evil empire" and the arms race went on, some Americans worried about the possibility of a nuclear war. In November 1983 the ABC television network broadcast a movie that showed what might happen during and after a nuclear war. The film, *The Day After*, drew a huge audience and sparked debates about surviving such a war.

The film shows what the effects might be on a typical American community after the Soviet Union responds to a U.S. missile attack. A local doctor tries to help the survivors, but many people die from radiation poisoning. The people who live try to find some hope after the nuclear devastation. Overall, *The Day After* is bleak; unlike most made-for-TV movies, there is no happy ending. Some conservatives criticized the film for this negative view, saying it would make Americans less supportive of Reagan's strong stance against the Soviet Union. Some anti-nuclear groups said the film was not negative enough in showing what would happen after a nuclear war.

New Strains in the Relationship

Star Wars and the lack of progress in arms talks strained U.S-Soviet relations. Andropov attacked Reagan's attitude toward the East, calling him "irresponsible." Reagan continued his own tough talk against the Russians. The United States also began flying more spy missions along the Soviet border. Said one Soviet air force pilot, "We were flying more often as there were more spy planes provoking us. We were in a constant state of tension."

That tension may have played a part in a major mistake by the Soviet military. On September 1, 1983, a South Korean airliner strayed off its course and entered Soviet airspace. A Soviet jet tried

---

to force the plane away. The crew of the Korean plane did not respond to messages from the Soviet aircraft. Some Soviet officials later claimed the Korean plane was on a spy mission of some kind. (That night a U.S. military plane was actually on a mission not far from the Korean plane.) Finally the Soviet jet fired a missile, shooting down the Korean plane. All 269 people on board were killed.

The United States immediately denounced the act. Reagan called it a "crime against humanity." Further statements by Reagan and his advisors stirred U.S. public opinion against the Soviet Union. Soviet leaders refused to admit they had made a mistake. They insisted that the plane was on a spy mission, even after they found that the aircraft was not a spy plane.

Tensions rose again in October after the United States invaded the Caribbean island of Grenada. The new government there was friendly with Cuba, and Cuban military advisors were on the island. President Reagan said a new landing strip built on Grenada was designed for large Soviet cargo planes. Grenadan leaders said the strip had actually been built so large passenger planes carrying tourists could land. Still, Reagan believed that the Soviet Union and Cuba planned to use Grenada "as a major military [base] to export terrorism and undermine democracy." The U.S. attack was meant to prevent this.

U.S. forces quickly took control of the island and put in a pro-American government. Most foreign countries condemned the invasion, but most Americans supported it. To Soviet leaders, the Grenada attack was another sign of Reagan's readiness to use military force.

The next month the Soviet Union received another jolt when NATO held military exercises in Europe. The training session was supposed to prepare NATO forces for possible actions during a nuclear war. These exercises, coming so soon after the Korean Air Lines (KAL) incident and Grenada, made Andropov and other Soviet leaders nervous. They worried that Reagan might be considering some kind of military move—even a nuclear attack— against their country.

Word of the Soviet fears reached Reagan. He decided that it was time to calm Andropov's concerns. Early in 1984 Reagan said he wanted to "avoid war and reduce the level of arms" and engage in "constructive cooperation" with the Soviet Union. His current secretary of state, George Shultz, held talks with Soviet foreign minister Andrei Gromyko. The talks seemed to go well.

Around this time Andropov died. The Soviet Communist party replaced him with Konstantin Chernenko, the third Soviet leader in three years. But even as he took the post, Chernenko's health was poor. He would serve barely a year before he, too, died in office. America would now see a new generation of Communist leaders emerge in the Soviet Union, led by Mikhail Gorbachev.

Espionage ☆   SPIES ON ALERT

Starting in May 1981, Yuri Andropov ordered his KGB agents to be extra alert for signs of a possible U.S. nuclear attack on the Soviet Union. Reagan's harsh Cold War language had already stirred Soviet concern. The agents stationed in NATO countries looked for certain activities that might indicate that the West was preparing for war. These preparations might include military personnel regularly working late hours, reserve soldiers being called up for duty, and blood banks being set up.

The KGB monitoring continued when Andropov became the Soviet leader. After the 1983 KAL incident and Grenada invasion, the KGB sent a message to its agents warning them of a U.S. attack. The United States and its allies learned about the Soviet warning from a double agent, Oleg Gordievsky. A KGB agent working in Moscow, Gordievsky was also passing secrets to British intelligence officers. At first the British did not believe Gordievsky's claim that the Soviet Union was preparing for a nuclear attack. Gordievsky said to them, "[Okay], I'll get you the documents!" William Casey, director of the CIA, eventually flew to London to talk to Gordievsky. The Americans now realized how nervous the Soviet leaders were. The information from Gordievsky helped convince Reagan to work toward better relations with the Soviet Union.

7

A NEW ERA

During the early 1980s, the Soviet Union replaced one aging leader with another. The West, meanwhile, was trying to learn something about the new generation of Soviet leaders waiting to come to power. In 1984 British prime minister Margaret Thatcher's government contacted a few of these younger Communist leaders, inviting them to visit Great Britain. The first one to accept the invitation was Mikhail Gorbachev.

Gorbachev surprised the British by taking his wife, Raisa, on the trip. Soviet leaders almost never traveled abroad with their wives. Gorbachev also seemed better-educated than some past Soviet leaders, with a more engaging personality. After Thatcher spent time with him, she said, "I like Mr. Gorbachev.

Mikhail Gorbachev and his wife Raisa (center) meet British prime minister Margaret Thatcher.

We can do business together." Thatcher's positive reaction to Gorbachev helped convince the Americans that he was someone with whom they could do business, too. They got their chance in March 1985, when Gorbachev became general secretary of the Communist party.

Glasnost and Perestroika

Segment #7
Glasnost and Perestroika

United States officials had their first chance to meet Gorbachev at the funeral of Konstantin Chernenko. Vice President George Bush and Secretary of State George Shultz were part of the American delegation. Shultz said to Bush about Gorbachev, "This is a very different Soviet leader than any we've seen before!"

Gorbachev had already indicated what kind of policies he would promote as leader of the Soviet Union. In December 1984 he gave a speech to Communist party officials. He discussed two new concepts: glasnost and perestroika. *Glasnost* means "openness." Gorbachev said that the Soviet government had to tell some of the truth to its citizens: "Frank information is evidence of confidence in the people and respect for their intelligence and feelings." *Perestroika* means "restructuring": The Communist party had to change its methods to improve the social and economic structure of the country. Gorbachev later said, "The state of the Soviet Union and its society could be described very simply with a phrase used by people across the country, 'We can't go on living like this any longer!'"

The Cold War and the arms race continued to cripple the Soviet economy. Gorbachev saw two clear choices: He could cut back on the production of consumer goods, which would further deprive his people. Or he could try to end the conflict with the West so that the Soviet Union could spend less money on weapons and more on the people. Once in power Gorbachev pursued glasnost, perestroika, and the easing of tensions with the United States. Gorbachev did not want to end communism in the Soviet Union, but he wanted to drastically change it.

Soon after taking office, Gorbachev made plans to meet with President Reagan. The leaders held their summit in Geneva, Switzerland, in November 1985. Before that, Shultz held meetings with the new Soviet foreign minister, Eduard Shevardnadze. The two sides laid out their positions. The Soviet Union wanted to cut all strategic nuclear warheads by 50 percent. Shevardnadze also wanted a ban on the development of space-based weapons. But the Americans refused to consider giving up SDI.

When Gorbachev and Reagan met, they argued about the ongoing arms race and each other's involvement in conflicts around the world. Reagan pushed for Star Wars, saying he would give the Soviet military the technology as the Americans developed it. This way the Soviet Union would not be left behind and feel open to a surprise attack. Gorbachev did not believe him. At one point during the summit, Gorbachev told other Soviet officials, "I have met a caveman—a dinosaur!" But at least the two sides were talking, and there seemed to be some hope for future arms reductions. A picture taken at the summit showed the two men smiling as they chatted in front of a fire. Reagan and Gorbachev also agreed that "a nuclear war cannot be won and must never be fought."

People ★ MIKHAIL GORBACHEV

As leader of the Soviet Union, Mikhail Gorbachev reformed the government and made serious proposals for arms reduction. His policies earned the respect of many Americans and Europeans. At home, however, some Communists opposed his reforms, saying they were too drastic. At the same time, many people wanted even greater reforms than Gorbachev was willing to make. Today, many Russians still blame him for the problems their country has faced since the end of the Cold War.

Gorbachev was born in the village of Privolnoye, Russia, on March 2, 1931. In the early 1950s, he joined the Communist party and earned a law degree. When he entered government service, he led the agriculture department in Stavropol Kray, a fertile region in southernmost Russia, east of the Black Sea. Major Communist leaders in Moscow, including Yuri Andropov, noticed Gorbachev's skills and helped him rise through the party ranks. Gorbachev came to Moscow and began handling agricultural affairs for the entire country.

When Gorbachev came to power in 1985, he introduced the policies of perestroika and glasnost. These were designed to improve the economy, lessen the complete power of the Communist party, and allow more contact with the West. Gorbachev also allowed the Eastern European satellite countries and some Soviet republics to pursue reform. This policy led to the end of Communist rule throughout Eastern Europe in 1989 and 1990. For his efforts Gorbachev won the 1990 Nobel Peace Prize.

In August 1991 Soviet Communists who opposed Gorbachev's reforms tried to reestablish strict party control. The support of some Soviet military units and public protests helped Gorbachev stay in power, but his political influence was weak. On December 25, 1991, he resigned as president of the Soviet Union. The next day the Soviet Union was officially dissolved, with its 15 republics forming separate countries.

Sources ★ THE FIRST REAGAN-GORBACHEV SUMMIT

Donald Regan served as an advisor to President Reagan from 1985 to 1987. He attended the November 1985 Geneva summit and had these observations.

We of course were always wary that…what Gorbachev might be trying to sell us might be exactly what we shouldn't want to buy. That we should try to stand up for what we wanted, and if he didn't like what we were doing…then it was all right to continue on that road, because anything that was to our advantage and to his disadvantage was something we wanted to pursue.…

In the famous fireside chat, the two had really gotten to know each other, and…they let it all hang out.… And neither one took offense when there were disagreements. And when there were agreements they stuck to them.…

[Afterward, Reagan] said that Gorbachev was a likable person, that he had a good personality, that he was forceful, he held his positions.… He was the type of person that might be convinced that if he thought we were on the level, he could be on the level.

A Bumpy Road to Arms Reduction

Despite the good will of the Geneva summit, Cold War attitudes did not change overnight. Soon after Geneva, Gorbachev made a bold proposal for nuclear arms reduction. Both sides, he said, should eliminate all their weapons by the year 2000. He also wanted the Soviet Union and the United States to stop nuclear testing and immediately remove their intermediate-range missiles from Europe. U.S. and Western European leaders considered the proposal to be mere propaganda and did not take it seriously.

Around the same time, the United States took some actions that seemed threatening to Soviet interests. A U.S. spy ship sailed into Soviet waters on a mission. U.S. jets bombed Libya, a Soviet ally in northern Africa, because of that country's alleged involvement in a terrorist attack. And Reagan continued to provide support for "freedom fighters" who opposed authoritarian governments, especially the mujahedeen in Afghanistan.

In March 1986 the president approved $300 million in *covert*, or secret, aid to the Afghan rebels. Said CIA agent Frank Anderson, "The amount of weaponry that was going in went up about ten times, between 1985 and 1986." The Soviet Union responded by using heavily armed helicopters, called gun ships. Fighting from the air, Soviet troops could more easily attack the mujahedeen and disrupt supply routes. The U.S. government then gave the mujahedeen a new weapon—the Stinger. This *antiaircraft* missile could shoot down the gun ships. Said Anderson, "The introduction of the Stinger missiles in one swoop drove back the helicopter gun ships...and that had a dramatic effect on [the mujahedeen's] morale and their efficiency and had a corresponding dramatic negative effect on the Soviet morale and efficiency."

Even before the Stingers arrived, Gorbachev had been trying to find a way for the Soviet Union to get out of Afghanistan without losing influence there. He said, "We had to finish this war, but in such a way that the Russian people would understand why tens of thousands had died.... [W]e couldn't just run away in shame." But it would take three more years before the Soviet Union pulled out. Meanwhile, the Soviet Union lost more soldiers and spent money that could have gone into the Soviet economy.

The Afghanistan war offered the first major battlefield test of the Stinger missile. This *surface-to-air missile* (SAM) is fired from a small launch tube that sits on a soldier's shoulder. The entire system weighs about 35 pounds (15.8 kg), making the Stinger easy to carry and fire. The missile itself is about five feet (1.52 m) long, weighs 12.5 pounds (5.7 kg), and can reach speeds of more than 1,000 miles (1,609 km) per hour.

The Stinger is called a "fire-and-forget" SAM. Its guidance system picks up on heat created by its target—a low-flying plane or helicopter. Once soldiers fire the Stinger, they can quickly take cover, since they do not have to control the missile's flight.

In Afghanistan the Soviet Union had to change its tactics once the mujahedeen received Stingers from the United States. By flying at higher altitudes, the gun ship pilots stayed out of the missiles' range, which is about 3 miles (4.8 km). But at the higher altitudes, the gun ships were not able to inflict as much damage. The mujahedeen used the Stinger to shoot down more than 250 Soviet aircraft. Since the late 1980s the U.S. government has improved the Stinger and released different versions of it. The Stinger is expected to remain part of the U.S. arsenal until the 2010s.

Places CHERNOBYL

While Mikhail Gorbachev was trying to reduce nuclear weapons, he was faced with a nuclear crisis of a different kind. On April 26, 1986, at the Chernobyl power plant in Ukraine, a nuclear reactor exploded. The explosion and resulting fires killed 31 people and released huge amounts of radiation into the air. Over time this radiation

A volunteer helping with the cleanup at the Chernobyl power plant

killed thousands more. Chernobyl was the worst accident ever at a nuclear power plant.

Gorbachev waited weeks before publicly talking about the accident. This silence was typical—Soviet leaders never liked to discuss the country's technical disasters. But after monitors in Sweden picked up unusually large amounts of radiation coming from the Soviet Union, Gorbachev admitted the accident. Even then Soviet leaders were slow to discuss full details or to act quickly to lessen the damage. Eventually more than 130,000 people were forced to leave their homes near the plant. Most were never allowed to return.

The Chernobyl accident showed how unprepared the Soviet Union was for a disaster of this kind. It also raised questions about Soviet technical standards. Although it was a high price to pay, Chernobyl helped reinforce Gorbachev's belief that the Soviet system had to change.

Breakthrough in Reykjavik

Gorbachev and Reagan pose at the Reykjavik summit.

After five years of pursuing his arms buildup, Reagan felt that he could negotiate with the Soviet Union from a position of strength. On the other side, Gorbachev felt an increasing need to end the arms race. In October 1986 the two leaders met at a quickly arranged summit in Reykjavik, Iceland.

Gorbachev was not ready to sign an agreement with Reagan, but he wanted to lay out his plans for arms reduction. On the first day, he called for reducing strategic nuclear weapons—ICBMs and intermediate-range missiles. The Americans were open to discussing these cuts. On the second day, Gorbachev went even further. He proposed the two sides get rid of all their intermediate-range weapons in Europe. Reagan had suggested this so-called "zero option" a few years before, but then the Soviet Union rejected it. Reagan was glad Gorbachev now seemed ready to accept it.

As the talks went on, each side made proposals for even larger cuts. They agreed to reduce their ICBMs and SLBMs by 50 percent over a five-year period. Then Gorbachev said both countries should eliminate all strategic nuclear weapons within ten years. According to Donald Regan, Reagan hit the table and said, "'Well, why didn't you say so in the first place! That's exactly what I [want to] do and if you [want to] do away with all the weapons, I'll agree to do away with all the weapons!"

Reagan called the new proposal "breathtaking" and later said, "George [Shultz] and I couldn't believe what was happening. We were getting amazing agreements. As the day went on, I felt something momentous was occurring." Reagan suggested that they include all nuclear weapons, both strategic and tactical. Gorbachev quickly agreed. But then the Soviet leader threw an obstacle into the path of the negotiations. All the agreements, he said, were based on Reagan's limiting research on Stars Wars. Gorbachev later said, "[M]y principal position was and remains the same. The nuclear arms race should never be taken into space. It was difficult enough to limit the nuclear arms race on Earth."

Gorbachev's demand surprised Reagan. Jack Matlock, an advisor on the National Security Council, said Reagan "reacted as if he had been asked to toss his favorite child into an erupting volcano." As eager as he was for arms reduction, Reagan would not give up SDI, and he broke off the meeting. Still, neither side saw the Reykjavik summit as a failure. The two sides had shown a new willingness to make deep arms cuts. Reagan said, "The significance of that meeting…is that we got as close as we did" to reaching an agreement.

Sources REAGAN & GORBACHEV AT REYKJAVIK

SDI was a major issue at Reykjavik. Here are excerpts taken from conversations between Ronald Reagan and Mikhail Gorbachev on that topic.

Reagan: *First, you are concerned that defense could be used for offense. I can assure you that is not the purpose of SDI.…*

Second, you voiced concern that the United States might obtain a possibility for carrying out a first strike and then avoid retaliation owing to defense. I can say that we do not have the capability for carrying out a first strike, and that this is not our goal.…

We are ready to share our accomplishments in strategic defense, and we could include a provision in the treaty which would make the quantity of defensive weapons deployed dependent upon the number of ballistic missiles remaining. Such a situation would be distinguished by high stability, since bombers and cruise missiles are unsuited to a surprise attack.…

We naturally need to examine the time and stages of transition to strategic defense. The principles of equality and stability would be observed at each stage in this process in this case. My proposal is a serious step, and we need to conduct serious negotiations.…

Gorbachev: *Excuse me, Mr. President, but I do not take your idea of sharing SDI seriously. You don't want to share even petroleum equipment, automatic machine tools, or equipment for dairies, while sharing SDI would be a second American Revolution. And revolutions do not occur all that often. Let's be realistic and pragmatic. That's more reliable.*

Reagan: *If I thought that SDI could not be shared, I would have rejected it myself.…*

It appears that the point is that I am the oldest man here. And I understand that after the [first world] war the nations decided that they would renounce poison gases. But thank

God the gas mask continued to exist. Something similar can happen with nuclear weapons. And we will have to shield against them in any case.

Gorbachev: *I am increasingly convinced of something I knew previously only second-hand. The President of the United States does not like to retreat.... So I see that the possibilities of agreement are exhausted.*

Real Reductions

In early 1987 Gorbachev kept up the efforts for significant arms cuts. He again proposed that both sides eliminate all intermediate-range nuclear weapons in Europe. He was willing to exclude British and French weapons, and he did not mention Star Wars. The Americans agreed. On December 8, 1987, the two sides signed the Intermediate-range Nuclear Force (INF) treaty. For the first time ever, each side agreed to get rid of an entire class of missiles. The Soviet Union would remove its SS-20s, while the Americans would pull out their Pershing IIs and cruise missiles. Each side also agreed to let the other verify that the weapons were destroyed. Gorbachev came to Washington, D.C., to sign the INF treaty, and the U.S. Senate approved it in May 1988.

Later that May Reagan made his first trip ever to Moscow. He walked the streets and met Soviet citizens. At one point a journalist asked Reagan if he thought he was visiting an "evil empire." Reagan said no: "I was talking about another time and another era." Gorbachev's reforms had created a totally different Soviet Union. But despite Reagan's change of heart and his warm relations with Gorbachev, the Americans still did not accept Soviet offers for reducing conventional military forces in Europe. And Reagan still would not abandon SDI.

In December 1988 Gorbachev returned to the United States to speak at the UN. Gorbachev showed that his desire for change was still strong. He said the Soviet Union would not wait for the United States to agree to reduce conventional forces. On its own, the Soviet Union was ready to cut its military forces by 500,000 troops. They would also remove 10,000 tanks, 8,500 artillery guns, and 800 combat planes from Eastern Europe.

That same day Gorbachev had one last meeting with Reagan. A new American president, George Bush, was preparing to take office. Reagan and Gorbachev had started a new era in U.S.-Soviet relations. No one could have predicted that so many important changes could have occurred in such a short time. Now, Gorbachev would continue his push for major reforms, taking new steps toward ending the Cold War.

Culture ☆ GLASNOST IN ACTION

Gorbachev's greatest successes came in foreign affairs. At home his policies of glasnost and perestroika had mixed results. Many Communists resisted his political and economic reforms. They also feared the *ethnic nationalism* that arose in some Soviet republics. This nationalism was particularly strong in the Baltic republics of Lithuania, Latvia, and Estonia. Still, the Soviet Union opened up as it never had before.

The changes were partially the result of new technologies spreading across the Soviet Union, such as fax machines and personal computers. Soviet citizens found it easier to get information that did not come from government sources. Gorbachev helped the process by giving the official media

more freedom. Books, plays, and films that had been banned could now be released. Historians had more freedom to tell the truth about the worst parts of earlier Soviet rule. And political dissidents, such as Anatoly Shcharansky, won their freedom.

Young people also enjoyed the freedoms of glasnost. They had easier access to rock and punk music, and they began openly to dress in the most outrageous Western styles. Some older people disliked these changes. But Andrei Pavlov, a student, said, "The main achievement of Gorbachev's policies was that, in the space of a year or two, he made the fear disappear, as if by magic. People had lost their fear of speaking and acting freely."

8

THE
END
OF THE
COLD WAR

George Bush, the new U.S. president in 1989, took a cautious approach to the changes Mikhail Gorbachev had brought to his country and to Soviet-American relations. "The Cold War isn't over," he had said as vice president in 1988, when Reagan visited Moscow. As president, Bush and his advisors took a few months to assess Gorbachev and his policies before making any bold moves.

At the same time, dramatic changes were beginning in Eastern Europe. Early in 1989 the Hungarian government prepared to hold free elections with many parties participating, not just the Communist party. Miklos Nemeth, the Hungarian prime minister, visited Gorbachev. He recalled Gorbachev's reaction to the Hungarian elections: "'I don't agree with the multi-party system…in Hungary, but that's not my responsibility, that's your responsibility. There will be no instruction or order by us to crush it down.'" In May the Hungarian government tore down the fence of barbed wire that marked its border with Austria. This was the first destruction of part of the "iron curtain" that had separated Eastern and Western Europe for 40 years.

A Hungarian soldier cuts the barbed wire fence
that separates his country from Austria.

Gorbachev's reaction to events in Hungary let all of Eastern Europe know that he would not block reforms. Poland soon followed, as General Wojciech Jaruzelski began holding talks with Lech Walesa and Solidarity. In partly free elections held in June, Solidarity won 99 out of 100 seats in the upper house of the Polish parliament. The party also took all of the seats it was allowed to run for in the lower house of the parliament. But not all the Soviet satellite states welcomed the changes that were underway.

People — GEORGE BUSH

During his 1988 presidential campaign, George Bush vowed to continue the policies begun by Ronald Reagan. He had served as Reagan's vice president since 1981 and seen firsthand the changes in U.S-Soviet relations. Bush welcomed the changes going on in the Soviet Union and its satellites. When the Soviet Union broke apart in 1991, Bush was able to tell America that the Cold War was completely over.

George Bush was born on June 12, 1924, in Milton, Massachusetts. His father, Prescott, was a wealthy businessman and served as a U.S. senator from Connecticut. George Bush headed to Texas to make his own fortune in the oil business. He entered local Republican politics in 1962. Two years later Bush ran for the U.S. Senate but lost. In 1966 he won a seat in the U.S. House of Representatives.

In 1971 Richard Nixon named Bush the U.S. ambassador to the UN. His later government posts included head of the CIA and chief U.S. representative to China. In 1980 Bush first ran for the Republican presidential nomination and then accepted Ronald Reagan's offer to run as vice president. Eight years later Bush won his own presidential election.

As president, Bush faced a major test in the Middle East. Iraq—led by Saddam Hussein—invaded neighboring Kuwait in August 1990. Bush won wide support among members of the UN to use an international force to drive the

Iraqis out of Kuwait. The Persian Gulf War in early 1991 lasted only six weeks, as the U.S. military led a decisive victory over Iraq. Bush was sometimes criticized for not removing Saddam, a brutal dictator, from power. But Bush insisted that the war was meant only to restore Kuwait's freedom.

In 1992 Bush lost his race for reelection to Bill Clinton. From then on, Bush largely avoided politics and public attention.

Resisting Reform

Romania's Nicolae Ceausescu and East Germany's Erich Honecker led the opposition to the reforms in Poland and Hungary. Both men believed in strict Communist rule and were not willing to share power with non-Communists. Gorbachev had once told all the Eastern European leaders that they needed to decide how to carry out perestroika. Gorbachev said that Honecker replied, "'We've done our perestroika, we have nothing to restructure.'"

Honecker had come to power as an opponent of change. He had created an image of economic progress for his country by making financial deals with West Germany. But the people lived in fear of the *Stasi*, East Germany's secret police, and were denied any freedom. Now, Honecker was especially threatened by the Hungarian reforms.

Many East Germans were trying to flee the country through Hungary. According to a treaty Hungary had signed with East Germany, the Hungarians were not supposed to let East Germans travel through Hungary to the West. But starting in September 1989, the Hungarians let the East Germans cross over into Austria. Thousands of East Germans quickly took advantage of this route to freedom. When East Germany then blocked travel to Hungary, East Germans went to Czechoslovakia instead. They flocked to the West German embassy there, seeking to get into West Germany. Honecker then closed the East German border with Czechoslovakia.

East German resistance to Honecker and communism continued to grow. Each Monday protesters gathered outside a church in the city of Leipzig. The crowd grew each week. They taunted the Stasi agents who watched them: "Stasi down, Stasi down...Stasi into the coal mines." The people also called out, "We are staying here." Instead of leaving East Germany, they were going to stay and reform it. "That was a turning point," said one protester, "and people said, 'We still have hope.'"

Protesters flee Beijing's Tiananmen Square as Chinese troops fire on them, ending the 1989 call for reform in Communist China.

★ Places — TIANANMEN SQUARE

While Mikhail Gorbachev was pushing for reform in the Soviet Union, the Communist leaders of China clung to many of their old ways. Under the rule of Deng Xiaoping, the Chinese had made important economic reforms, especially in agriculture. But Deng and other leaders refused to lessen the Communist party's tight control over the government. In the spring of 1989, hundreds of thousands of Chinese students and workers came to Beijing's

Tiananmen Square to protest this lack of political reform.

Tiananmen Square is a huge public space in the center of China's capital. It borders the Great Hall of the People, where many government events are held. In the center of Tiananmen Square is the tomb of Mao Zedong, China's first Communist leader. The Chinese government often uses the square for rallies attended by up to 500,000 people. But in the protests of 1989, Tiananmen Square was the center of pro-democracy demonstrations and speeches.

As the protests grew, the Communist party leaders decided that they had to act. On June 4 tanks rolled into the area around Tiananmen Square, followed by troops. In the shooting that followed, hundreds of protesters were killed. Thousands more were arrested. The Tiananmen Square massacre unfolded as Western television crews broadcast the scene.

In East Germany, Erich Honecker supported the Chinese crackdown against its own people. He and other Eastern European leaders favored using similar tactics against protesters in their own countries. But with the Soviet Union opposing such extreme measures, only limited force was used.

The Wall Falls

Segment #8
The Wall Falls

In October 1989 Gorbachev and the leaders of the other Warsaw Pact countries met in Berlin, East Germany. They came to celebrate the fortieth anniversary of East Germany's founding. In the streets, people chosen by the East German government held a welcoming rally. But instead of shouting slogans in praise of their government, they chanted, "Gorby, Gorby, save us." Gorbachev—"Gorby"—heard the shouts, but Honecker ignored them. In meetings with Gorbachev, the East German leader insisted that he had events under control, and he would not pursue a German version of perestroika. Gorbachev told him, "He who lags behind events, loses." Gorbachev saw that Honecker could not survive for long.

The Leipzig demonstrations continued, and army units were put on call. Said one protester, "There was permanent fear that there might be a 'Chinese solution' to the problem and that weapons might be used." Honecker wanted to use force, but Soviet leaders refused to support him. Within the national government, Honecker was under attack. He was finally replaced by Egon Krenz, who reluctantly backed some reform. Krenz promised to allow East Germans to travel freely to the West. However, the people began to demand even more. On November 4, 500,000 people held a rally in East Berlin. The government wanted to reform socialism, but the people were calling for democracy.

On November 9 the East German government announced that starting the next day, it would allow people to get visas for travel to the West. But the official order was unclear, and border guards began opening the gates and letting people pass through. For the first time in almost 30 years, thousands of people crossed

freely into West Berlin. Said one East Berliner, "I found myself in a group of people who were applauding.... I realized I was in West Berlin.... We were all crying and embracing each other."

West Berliners rushed to greet the people who poured through the gates. They also began to attack the wall with hammers and chisels, trying to bring it down. Television cameras showed the world this emotional end of an era from

A West Berliner helps tear down the Berlin Wall.

the Cold War. In Moscow, Gorbachev thought that the East German government had made the right decision, "because how could you shoot at Germans who walk across the border to meet Germans on the other side[?]" In the United States, George Bush tried not to overreact, saying simply, "I am very pleased with this development."

Meeting in Malta

In December 1989 Bush and Gorbachev held their first summit. They met on a ship docked at Malta, an island in the Mediterranean Sea. The meeting had been planned during the summer. Eastern Europe had changed dramatically since then. Poland and Hungary were no longer ruled by Communists. The Berlin Wall was coming down, and East Germany was making major reforms in its government. Bulgaria was also making reforms. In Czechoslovakia a bloodless "Velvet" Revolution in late November had led to the collapse of communism. Soon after, dissident Vaclav Havel rose to the presidency.

The Malta summit got off to a rough start—literally. Stormy seas tossed the boats in the harbor. After some delay the two leaders finally met. Bush started by telling Gorbachev, "The world will be a better place if perestroika succeeds." The president wanted to give the Soviet Union economic aid. He also pushed for more START negotiations. The meetings went well, though the two leaders disagreed about Cuba's military involvement in Central America. Gorbachev insisted that he could not control Castro. No new agreements were signed in Malta, but the mood was positive. Said Gorbachev, "Malta was the place, where for the first time, we said we no longer considered each other enemies."

Gorbachev's international prestige was still high, but at home he faced some problems. The Baltic republics of Lithuania, Latvia, and Estonia wanted their independence. These three republics had been free states from 1918 until 1940, when they were taken over by the Soviet Union. The Baltic peoples had always opposed Soviet rule. Gorbachev was reluctant to recognize their independence. He claimed that if he did so, other republics would then clamor for independence, too.

Some Soviet citizens were also demanding changes in the Communist government. People protested in Moscow, and in early February, Gorbachev responded. He proposed ending the

Communist party's leading role in the government, a position guaranteed by the Soviet constitution. He also called for more economic reforms. Within the government, the forces that wanted to keep things the same argued with people who supported Gorbachev and those who wanted even more reform. The tensions increased in the months to come.

| **Places** | ROMANIA |

While most of the Soviet satellites made a peaceful change from communism to democracy, the situation was different in Romania in 1989. Its leader, Nicolae Ceausescu, ruled as a dictator and refused to give up any control.

Romania is located west of the Black Sea. It borders Bulgaria, Yugoslavia, Hungary, Ukraine, and Moldova. The Carpathian Mountains cover almost a third of the country, and the Danube River flows through Romania to the Black Sea. The capital is Bucharest.

Romania had fought with Germany against the Soviet Union during the first few years of World War II but then switched sides in 1944 to support the Allies. Soviet troops occupied the country after the war, and a Communist government was established in 1947. Ceausescu came to power in 1965.

Under him, all agriculture and industry were controlled by the state. Ceausescu used his secret police, the Securitate, to terrorize the people. His wife, Elena, helped him carry out his harsh rule. Both Ceausescus were deeply hated by most Romanians.

In late 1989 as reform swept through Eastern Europe, Ceausescu vowed to stay in power. In December the secret police fired on protesters in the city of Timisoara. Dozens were killed, but the protests grew, and Ceausescu finally decided to flee the country. He and his wife were caught and arrested by the government that replaced them. On December 25, the Ceausescus were executed. The Romanian government came under the control of other Communists, who carried out some minor reforms. The Communists were voted out of office in 1996.

A Time of Constant Change

In March 1990 Lithuania and Estonia proclaimed their independence from the Soviet Union. Latvia followed in May. Gorbachev felt pressure to react, though he had promised Bush that he would not use force in the Baltics. Instead, Gorbachev took economic steps, cutting off almost all oil and gas supplies to Lithuania.

At the end of May, Gorbachev faced tough issues both at home and abroad. Boris Yeltsin was elected leader of the Russian parliament. He called for increasing independence for the Russian Republic, the largest in the Soviet Union. Foreign Minister Shevardnadze said, "Gorbachev would never really acknowledge that the Soviet Union would break up. Yeltsin realized that it was inevitable...and he was one of the first to take the initiative."

In East Germany the new leaders were planning to reunite with West Germany as a democratic country. At first Gorbachev demanded that a unified Germany be neutral. The Russians still had bitter memories of World War II, and for most of the Cold War, they had struggled to eliminate any future military threats from Germany. But Gorbachev finally decided that he did not have the power to keep a unified Germany out of NATO. West Germany was the stronger of the two Germanys, and it would set the policies for the new state. Condoleeza Rice was an aide to Bush in Soviet affairs. She said, "The agreement between Gorbachev and [West German leader Helmut] Kohl...was the end of the Cold War."

As the year went on, changes continued within the Soviet Union. More republics declared their independence. The Soviet government allowed freedom of religion and multi-party elections. Yeltsin kept fighting to weaken the power of the central government. In October the Russian Republic and Ukraine declared that their state laws now outweighed the laws of the Soviet Union. Gorbachev tried to keep the Soviet Union together while trying to give the individual republics more self-rule.

A Soviet tank rolling through the Lithuanian capital of Vilnius.

Meanwhile, tensions kept building in the Baltics. On January 2, 1991, Gorbachev sent troops into the Lithuanian capital of Vilnius and the Latvian capital of Riga. Their mission was to occupy government buildings in the two cities. As the month went on, elite Soviet troops clashed with protesters, killing 14 people in Lithuania and 5 in Latvia. Gorbachev backed down from using any more violence even as some Communists in his government called for a larger crackdown. These conservatives were losing patience with Gorbachev and his reforms.

People   BORIS YELTSIN

In the last days of the Soviet Union, Boris Yeltsin emerged as a hero. In the summer of 1991, he led the protests that kept Mikhail Gorbachev in power. Then, Yeltsin worked to ensure that the Soviet republics earned their independence. But as the Russian president, Yeltsin had a mixed record. His ill health and poor decision-making sometimes hurt his ability to govern effectively.

Yeltsin was born on February 1, 1931, in Sverdlovsk (now Ekaterinburg), Russia. Trained as a construction engineer, he joined the Communist party when he was 30. When Gorbachev came to power in 1985, he named Yeltsin the head of the Moscow Communist party. Yeltsin quickly began to reform the local party and pushed for a faster pace for perestroika. His efforts went beyond what the party leadership wanted, and he was stripped of his post in 1987. Three years later Yeltsin quit the Communist party.

Still a strong supporter of reform, Yeltsin was elected president of the Russian Republic in 1991. He was the first popularly elected leader in Russian history. A few months later, Yeltsin led the resistance against a *coup* attempt. Yeltsin's heroics guaranteed his popularity with the Russian people.

After the collapse of the Soviet Union, Yeltsin remained leader of the newly independent country of Russia.

He stayed on good terms with U.S. leaders, who welcomed his reforms. But at home Yeltsin had growing problems. Corruption and crime rose while the economy struggled. In 1994 the Russian president began a long, bloody war in Chechnya, a region of Russia seeking its independence. Yeltsin also suffered from heart problems and was often out of the public eye. Yeltsin was reelected president in 1996, but his support continued to weaken. On December 31, 1999, Yeltsin resigned and turned over the Russian presidency to Prime Minister Vladimir Putin.

Trouble by the Sea

During the summer of 1991, the Americans and Russians kept working on arms reduction. In June the two sides reached final agreement on the Conventional Forces in Europe (CFE) treaty. The initial treaty had been signed in November 1990. This pact limited the number of conventional weapons and troops each side would keep in Europe. The next month the United States and the Soviet Union signed the START I treaty. This agreement limited each side to 6,000 strategic nuclear weapons.

While these talks went on, trouble swirled around Gorbachev. In June his opponents tried to make him crack down on reform. In August they turned to force. Gorbachev was vacationing near the Black Sea. A group of *hard-line*, or conservative, Communists visited him, demanding that he declare a state of national emergency or resign. When Gorbachev refused to do either, they proceeded without him. The hard-liners hoped that he would eventually join their efforts. Some top government leaders, including Prime Minister Valentin Pavlov and KGB chairman Vladimir Kryuchkov, organized the coup.

In Moscow, Vice President Gennady Yaneyev declared that he and an Emergency Committee were now in control. Protesters, including Yeltsin, began to gather outside the White House, the Russian parliament building. Said one Moscow citizen, "We were defending a free Russia, and the symbol of free Russia was Yeltsin. We joined hands and waited for the tanks in dead silence." In one memo-

While standing on a tank, Yeltsin speaks to a crowd during a tense moment of the 1991 coup.

rable moment, Yeltsin climbed onto a tank to denounce the coup.

President Bush, meanwhile, said little publicly about the coup, waiting to see how events unfolded. In private he worried for Gorbachev's safety. "I felt that a friend was in real trouble, and God knows, might not get out of there alive."

But Yeltsin and the other defenders of the parliament building achieved a great victory. Some military commanders and government officials refused to follow the orders of the Emergency Committee. More protesters filled the streets. Within three days the hard-liners realized they could not hold power. When Gorbachev returned to Moscow, he said, "Everything we have achieved since 1985 has borne fruit. Society and our people have changed. It was this that stopped the coup from succeeding."

Although still the leader of the Soviet Union, Gorbachev was politically weak. Yeltsin now held the real power. He forced Gorbachev to announce on television that the plotters had been powerful members of the government. Gorbachev and the Communist party had lost respect. On August 24 Gorbachev resigned as head of the party. The party itself fell apart a few days later. Gorbachev was still the Soviet president and hoped to keep the country intact. He thought that perhaps the government could be set up like the United States, with a national government and state governments side by side. But Yeltsin, Russia, and the other republics would not accept this arrangement. The Soviet Union was in the process of collapsing.

Sources ☆ YELTSIN'S SPEECH

Here are excerpts from Boris Yeltsin's speech of August 19, 1991, delivered as he stood on a tank outside the Russian White House.

Citizens of Russia: On the night of 18–19 August 1991, the legally elected president of the country was removed from power.

Regardless of the reasons given for his removal, we are dealing with a[n]...unconstitutional coup....

We considered and consider that such methods of force are unacceptable. They discredit the union in the eyes of the whole world, undermine our prestige in the world community, and return us to the Cold War era along with the Soviet Union's isolation in the world community. All of this forces us to proclaim that the so-called [Emergency] committee's ascendancy to power is unlawful.

Accordingly we proclaim all decisions and instructions of this committee to be unlawful.

We are confident that the organs of local power will unswervingly adhere to constitutional laws and decrees of the president of Russia.

We appeal to citizens of Russia to give a fitting rebuff to the [plotters] and demand a return of the country to normal constitutional development....

Final Days

Segment
#9
Final Days
of the Iron
Curtain

Soon after the coup, some of the Soviet republics declared their independence. In November, Yeltsin's Russia took over the diplomatic functions of the Soviet Union. A month later Russia and the former republics of Belarus and Ukraine agreed to form a new, loose union of their countries, the Commonwealth of Independent States. Most of the other former republics joined this new government. Gorbachev realized the Soviet Union had broken apart for good. On December 25, 1991, he resigned as president of a country that officially ceased to exist a week later.

Shortly after Gorbachev resigned, President Bush made a Christmas broadcast to the American people. He said, "For over 40 years, the United States led the West in the struggle against communism and the threat it posed to our most precious values. This struggle shaped the lives of all Americans. It forced all nations to live under the specter of nuclear destruction. That confrontation is now over."

Since that day, historians and diplomatic experts have wondered if the Cold War had to be fought at all, or had to last so long. Gorbachev said, "The West exaggerated the strength of the Soviet Union. We could not possibly have moved into Europe [after World War II]." U.S. diplomat Paul Nitze said, "I can't imagine any circumstance under which we could have gotten along with Uncle Joe Stalin. I can imagine no circumstance under which we could have worked out our problems with Russia earlier than we did, or in a different way."

Historians have also tried to hand out credit for who ended the Cold War. Some praise Ronald Reagan and his tough stance against the Soviet Union during the 1980s. Others see Gorbachev's reforms as the crucial step. George Bush probably stated what some experts believe: "There is so much room for credit in something as big as the end of the Cold War."

The end of the Cold War did not eliminate all threats of armed conflict and possible nuclear war. But the ideological struggle between two great superpowers was over. And with that ending, a longstanding state of fear was gone, as well.

Time Line

OCTOBER 1964	Nikita Khrushchev is forced from power and replaced by Leonid Brezhnev; Communist China tests its first nuclear weapon.
MARCH 1965	U.S. ground troops arrive in South Vietnam.
JUNE 1967	The Six-Day War occurs between Israel and the Arab states of Egypt, Jordan, and Syria; President Lyndon B. Johnson and Soviet premier Aleksei Kosygin meet in the United States to discuss limiting antiballistic missiles (ABMs).
SPRING 1968	Czechoslovak leader Alexander Dubcek adopts reforms, initiating the "Prague Spring."
AUGUST 1968	Warsaw Pact troops invade Czechoslovakia (itself a member of the Warsaw Pact) and end the period of internal reform.
JANUARY 1969	Richard Nixon is sworn in as president of the United States.
NOVEMBER 1969	The Strategic Arms Limitation Talks (SALT) begin in Geneva, Switzerland.
AUGUST 1970	West German chancellor Willy Brandt signs a treaty with the Soviet Union recognizing the existence of East Germany as a separate state.
FEBRUARY 1972	Nixon visits China.
MAY 1972	Nixon visits the Soviet Union and signs nuclear arms control agreements.
AUGUST 1974	Nixon resigns; Gerald Ford is sworn in as president of the United States.
NOVEMBER 1974	Ford and Brezhnev hold arms reduction talks in Vladivostok, a city in the far east of the Soviet Union.
1975	The U.S. and the Soviet Union back opposing sides in the Angolan civil war.
JULY 1975	The U.S. and Soviet Union conduct a joint exercise in space during the Apollo-Soyuz Test Project.
AUGUST 1975	Leaders from 35 countries sign the Helsinki Accords, recognizing post-World War II European borders and promoting human rights.
JANUARY 1977	Jimmy Carter is sworn in as president of the United States.
SEPTEMBER 1978	Israel and Egypt sign peace accords at Camp David, Maryland.
JANUARY 1979	The United States begins official diplomatic ties with China.
JUNE 1979	Carter and Brezhnev sign the SALT II treaty.
SUMMER 1979	The Sandinistas take power in Nicaragua.
NOVEMBER 1979	The Iranian hostage crisis begins.
DECEMBER 1979	Soviet troops invade Afghanistan.
AUGUST 1980	The United States boycotts the Summer Olympics in Moscow.
JANUARY 1981	Ronald Reagan is sworn in as president of the United States.
DECEMBER 1981	The Communist government in Poland cracks down on Solidarity and introduces martial law.

1982	The U.S. and the Soviet Union begin Strategic Arms Reduction Talks (START) in Geneva.
NOVEMBER 1982	Leonid Brezhnev dies and is replaced by Yuri Andropov.
MARCH 1983	Reagan announces the Strategic Defense Initiative (SDI), also known as Star Wars.
MID-1984	Congress bans U.S. aid to the Contras, anti-Communist rebels fighting in Nicaragua.
MARCH 1985	Mikhail Gorbachev takes power in the Soviet Union.
APRIL 1986	An explosion and a fire at the Chernobyl nuclear power plant, in Ukraine, release huge amounts of deadly radiation.
OCTOBER 1986	Reagan and Gorbachev meet in Reykjavik, Iceland, to discuss arms reduction.
DECEMBER 1987	The United States and the Soviet Union agree to eliminate all intermediate-range nuclear forces (INF) in Europe.
DECEMBER 1988	Gorbachev speaks at the United Nations (UN) and announces large cuts in Soviet military forces stationed in Eastern Europe.
JANUARY 1989	George Bush is sworn in as president of the United States.
FEBRUARY 1989	The Soviet withdrawal from Afghanistan is completed on schedule.
JUNE 1989	The Chinese government massacres pro-democracy demonstrators near Tiananmen Square; Solidarity wins the first partly free elections in Poland since World War II.
NOVEMBER 1989	East Germans are allowed to travel freely to West Berlin; the Berlin Wall begins to come down, and the end of Communist rule is at hand; Communist reformers take power in Bulgaria; Czechoslovakia's "Velvet Revolution" ends Communist rule in that country.
DECEMBER 1989	Bush and Gorbachev meet in Malta; Nicolae Ceausescu is forced from power in Romania; he and his wife are executed.
AUGUST 1990	Iraq invades Kuwait.
OCTOBER 1990	East and West Germany reunite as one country.
JUNE 1991	Boris Yeltsin is elected by popular vote to the new position of president of Russia.
JULY 1991	U.S. and Soviet leaders sign the START I treaty in Moscow.
AUGUST 1991	Yeltsin helps defeat a hard-line coup attempt and emerges as the most powerful political figure in the Soviet Union.

The Baltic states establish their independence. |
| DECEMBER 1991 | A referendum in Ukraine results in an overwhelming vote for independence; Yeltsin and the leaders of Belarus and Ukraine sign a treaty ending the Soviet Union and form the Commonwealth of Independent States; other independent republics soon join; Gorbachev announces the end of all Soviet government functions and resigns. |

Glossary

antiaircraft—Having to do with weapons capable of shooting airplanes or other aircraft out of the sky.

antiballistic missile (ABM)—A missile designed to shoot down long-range nuclear missiles.

back channel—Secret contact between leaders of different governments.

broken arrow—U.S. military nickname for a missing or damaged nuclear weapon.

bureaucracy—Different levels of authority in a government or other large organization.

capitalism—An economic system that promotes free enterprise and private ownership of goods; individuals and companies, rather than the government, make most economic decisions.

censorship—Government actions to prevent the publication or distribution of information.

Central Intelligence Agency (CIA)—A U.S. government organization that gathers information about and sometimes influences events in foreign countries.

civil defense—Government policies and plans for protecting civilians during a nuclear war.

communism—A political system featuring one party that holds complete power and promotes socialism.

Communist bloc—A group of allied countries that follow communism.

conservative—A person who wants to hold on to traditional beliefs or policies.

conventional weapons—Arms that do not use nuclear energy for their destructive force.

counterattack—A military action in response to another country's first strike.

coup—The violent takeover of a government, often by the military.

covert—Hidden or secret.

czarist—Relating to the czar, the ruler of Russia before the 1917 revolution.

democracy—A government that is ruled by the citizens of a state, who vote on issues directly or elect representatives to decide issues for them.

deployment—The introduction of a weapon to a military force; the strategic placement of military troops and weapons.

détente—The easing of tensions.

deter—To prevent or stop.

diplomat—A government representative who negotiates with foreign governments.

dissident—A person who publicly disagrees with government policies.

espionage—The process of gathering secret information.

ethnic nationalism—The desire of people of a specific culture to establish their own independent nations.

fundamentalists—Religious believers who follow closely the teachings of a holy book, such as the Koran.

glasnost—Russian word meaning "openness"; relates to reforms begun in the Soviet Union after Mikhail Gorbachev came to power in 1985.

gulag—A Soviet prison camp where inmates were forced to work for the government.

hard-line—Referring to the strict acceptance of a government policy or theory.

Hot Line—A direct communications link between the president of the United States and leaders in the Soviet Union.

hydrogen bomb—A highly destructive weapon that gets its explosive force from nuclear fusion.

ideology—A set of basic beliefs that help shape attitudes or behavior.

intercontinental ballistic missile (ICBM)—A missile that can travel more than 3,500 miles (5,600 km)—from one continent to another—carrying one or more nuclear warheads.

intermediate-range ballistic missile—A nuclear missile with a shorter range than an ICBM, usually from about 1,500 to 3,500 miles (2,400 to 5,600 km).

iron curtain—The symbolic boundary between Western and Eastern Europe during the Cold War; also the actual barbed wire and other boundaries separating these two regions.

KGB—*Komitet Gosudarstvennoy Bezopasnosti:* Russian for "Committee for State Security"; after 1954, the name of the major Soviet spy agency.

Koran—The holy book of the Islamic religion.

laser—A powerful beam of light capable of damaging objects or people; now also used for certain surgical operations.

long-range ballistic missile—A nuclear missile that can travel more than 3,500 miles (5,600 km); see also *intercontinental ballistic missile.*

Marxist—Relating to the beliefs of German thinker Karl Marx, particularly his idea that workers should own factories and other sources of economic wealth.

massive retaliation—A U.S. strategy to respond to any Soviet attack with all possible military means, including nuclear force.

megaton—The explosive force of one million tons of TNT; a unit for measuring the power of a nuclear weapon.

military draft—The selection of civilians to serve as soldiers during war.

mujahedeen—Arabic for "holy warriors" or "soldiers of god"; name given to the Muslims who fought Soviet troops in Afghanistan.

multiple independently targeted reentry vehicle (MIRV)—Long-range nuclear missiles holding more than one bomb.

mutual assured destruction (MAD)—The condition that exists when two countries have enough nuclear weapons to both survive a surprise attack by each other and respond with devastating force.

neutron bomb—A nuclear weapon designed to kill using large doses of radiation.

nonaligned—Not openly supporting another country, especially either the United States or the Soviet Union during the Cold War.

North American Air Defense Command (NORAD)—A joint U.S. and Canadian military agency that watches for nuclear attacks.

North Atlantic Treaty Organization (NATO)—A military alliance of Western European countries, along with the United States and Canada.

nuclear—Relating to the core, or nucleus, of an atom; relating to weapons that use the energy produced by splitting atoms (fission) or combining atoms (fusion).

perestroika—Russian word meaning "restructuring"; relates to reforms begun in the Soviet Union after Mikhail Gorbachev came to power in 1985.

plutonium—A highly radioactive metal used to make nuclear weapons.

Politburo—The ruling body of the Soviet Communist party.

propaganda—Information spread by a state or group for the purpose of influencing others' thoughts, attitudes, or behavior in a specific way.

proxy—A person or group that acts for another person or group.

radiation—Energy released by matter as the result of the movement of atomic and subatomic particles; human beings are exposed to radiation all the time (light and radio waves being two common examples); however, exposure to radiation in high doses or from unusual sources—such as from the explosion of a nuclear weapon—can result in serious illness and death.

radioactive—Relating to the release of radiation.

reciprocity—The equal exchange of benefits or privileges between two countries.

refuseniks—Soviet Jewish citizens who were not allowed to leave the Soviet Union.

satellite—A country under the influence of a more powerful neighboring country; in space, a natural or artificial object that orbits a planet.

socialism—An economic system that features government ownership of businesses and a high degree of central control over economic decisions.

solidarity—The unity of members in a group who share similar beliefs and goals.

Stasi—The East German secret police force during the Cold War era.

Strategic Air Command (SAC)—During the Cold War, the U.S. Air Force unit responsible for the nation's fleet of nuclear bombers.

Strategic Arms Limitation Talks (SALT)—From 1969 to 1979, talks between U.S. and Soviet officials to limit the number of nuclear weapons built by each country.

Strategic Arms Reduction Talks (START)—Beginning in 1982, talks between U.S. and Soviet officials to reduce the number of nuclear weapons built by each country.

Strategic Defense Initiative (SDI)—A proposal by President Ronald Reagan to use space-based weapons to destroy nuclear missiles launched at the United States.

submarine-launched ballistic missile (SLBM)—A long-range nuclear missile launched from a submarine.

superpower—One of a small number of countries with a large military force and influence over other countries.

surface-to-air missile (SAM)—A missile launched from the ground at attacking aircraft.

tactical nuclear weapon—A small nuclear weapon designed to be used on a battlefield.

Taliban—An Islamic group that won control of most of Afghanistan during the mid-1990s.

thermonuclear weapon—Another name for a hydrogen bomb.

Third World country—During the Cold War, any nation of Latin America, Africa, or Asia unaligned with a superpower; today, the term denotes an underdeveloped or developing country.

Bibliography

The Associated Press Library of Disasters, vol. 8. *Nuclear and Industrial Disasters*. Danbury, CT: Grolier Educational, 1998.

Blum, John, et al. *The National Experience.* 4th ed. New York: Harcourt Brace Jovanovich, Inc., 1977.

Bullock, Alan, and Woodings, R.B. *20th Century Culture: A Biographical Companion.* New York: Harper & Row, 1983.

Foner, Eric, and Garraty, John A., eds. *The Reader's Companion to American History.* Boston: Houghton Mifflin, 1991.

Isaacs, Jeremy, and Downing, Taylor. *Cold War: An Illustrated History, 1945–1991.* Boston: Little, Brown and Company, 1998.

Paterson, Thomas G., Clifford, J. Garry, and Hagan, Kenneth J. *American Foreign Relations: A History, Volume II.* 5th ed. Boston: Houghton Mifflin, 2000.

Paterson, Thomas G., and Clifford, J. Garry. *America Ascendant: U.S. Foreign Relations Since 1939.* Lexington, Massachusetts: D.C. Heath and Company: 1995.

Paterson, Thomas G., and Merrill, Dennis, eds. *Major Problems in American Foreign Relations. Volume II: Since 1914.* Boston: Houghton Mifflin, 2000.

Shaw, Warren, and Pryce, David. *World Almanac of the Soviet Union.* New York: World Almanac, 1990.

Sontag, Sherry, and Drew, Christopher. *Blind Man's Bluff.* New York: HarperPaperbacks, 1999.

World Book Year Book, 1975. Chicago: Field Enterprises Educational Corporation, 1975.

World Book Year Book, 1982. Chicago: World Book, Inc., 1982.

Resources for Students

Books

Daniels, Robert V., ed. *A Documentary History of Communism in Russia: From Lenin to Gorbachev.* Burlington, VT: University of Vermont Press, 1993.

Gorbachev, Mikhail. *On My Country and the World.* Translated by George Shriver. New York: Columbia University Press, 1999.

Hill, Kenneth, ed. *Cold War Chronology: Soviet-American Relations, 1945–1991.* Washington, D.C.: Congressional Quarterly, 1993.

Levering, Ralph B. *The Cold War: A Post-Cold War History.* Arlington Heights, Illinois: Harlan Davidson, 1994.

Matlock, Jack F. *Autopsy on an Empire: The American Ambassador's Account of the Collapse of the Soviet Union.* New York: Random House, 1995.

Matthews, John R. *The Rise and Fall of the Soviet Union.* San Diego: Lucent Books, 2000.

Miller, Calvin Craig. *Boris Yeltsin: First President of Russia.* Greensboro, North Carolina: Morgan Reynolds, 1994.

Streissguth, Thomas. *Soviet Leaders from Lenin to Gorbachev.* Minneapolis: Oliver Press, 1992.

Warren, James A. *Cold War: The American Crusade Against the Soviet Union and Communism, 1945–1991.* New York: Lothrop, Lee & Shepard, 1996.

Websites

Centre for Defence and International Security Studies

http://www.cdiss.org

CDISS, the Centre for Defence and International Security Studies, is an interdisciplinary research center based in the Department of Politics and International Relations at Lancaster University in Great Britain. This site gives an overview of the Centre, its personnel, and its output, and provides access to material from their research activities and publications.

CNN Cold War

http://cnn.com/specials/cold.war

CNN Interactive online companion to the CNN Cold War 24-part series. Contains program summaries, transcripts of interviews, maps, historical documents, interactive games, and much more information on the Cold War.

Cold War International History Project

http://cwihp.si.edu

This site is home to a broad collection of primary source documents recently released from Eastern-bloc countries.

Cold War Museum

http://www.coldwar.org

This is an online web museum dedicated to the history of the Cold War. Provides background information, time lines, photographs, and useful links on the Cold War.

Cold War Policies 1945–1991

http://ac.acusd.edu/history/20th/coldwar.html

This site features an interactive outline of key Cold War Policies from 1945 to 1991. It is housed on the history department site of the University of San Diego.

Federation of American Scientists—The High Energy Weapons Archive

http://www.fas.org/nuke/hew/index.html

This site offers a guide to nuclear weapons, including background information, photographs, and time lines that detail the development and use of atomic weapons.

Harvard Project on Cold War Studies

http://www.fas.harvard.edu/~hpcws/

This site contains a wide range of recently declassified primary source documents on the Cold War. The HPCWS promotes archival research in former Eastern-bloc countries and seeks to expand and enrich what is known about Cold War events and themes.

Library of Congress Country Studies-The Soviet Union

http://rs6.loc.gov/frd/cs/soviet_union/su_appnc.html

This site contains an extensive essay on the background of the Warsaw Pact.

National Security Archive

http://www.gwu.edu/~nsarchiv

This site contains a broad range of declassified materials obtained under the Freedom of Information Act.

http://www.gwu.edu/~nsarchiv/coldwar/interviews

The complete set of interview transcripts used in the 24-part CNN Cold War series.

http://www.gwu.edu/~nsarchiv/coldwar/documents

The primary source documents referenced in the 24-part CNN Cold War series.

The Presidents of the United States

http://www.ipl.org/ref/POTUS/

This site is housed on the larger Internet Public Library for the Presidents of the United States. This site gives extensive background and links on George Bush, Jimmy Carter, Gerald Ford, Lyndon B. Johnson, John F. Kennedy, Richard Nixon, and Ronald Reagan.

Strategic Arms Reduction Treaty

http://bullatomsci.org/research/collections/armscntrlSTART.html

This special collection brings together articles from the *Bulletin of Atomic Scientists* related to the recent negotiation and ratification of agreements between the United States and Russia for reductions in intercontinental nuclear forces.

UCLA Army ROTC

http://www.sscnet.ucla.edu/milsci/branch/stinger.html

This site provides text on the Stinger missile.

U.S. News Online: Cold War Archive

http://www.usnews.com/usnews/news/991018/histarch.htm

This online companion to the *U.S. News and World Report* contains a collection of articles on Cold War history.

Videos

The Day After. Summa Video, 1995.

Red Star Rising. MPI, 1989.

The Rise and Fall of the Soviet Union. VCI Home Entertainment, 1992.

Index

Pages in italics indicate illustrations or maps.

ABM—see antiballistic missile

Afghanistan 4, 60, 62, *63*, 64–65, 66, 67–68, 73, 78, 82, 83, 94, 95, 116, 117, 120

Africa 9, *31*, 49, 57, 58, 67, 94, 121

Africa, Horn of 57, 58, 59

Allies 109

Amin, Hazifullah 63, 64, 66

Andropov, Yuri 66, 82, 83–84, 86, 87, 88, 92, 117

Angola *48–50, 58*

antiballistic missile (ABM) 31–32, 35, 36, 39, 116, 118

Apollo-Soyuz Test Project (ASTP) 44–*45*, 48, 116

Asia 9, 10, *31*, 121

ASTP—see Apollo-Soyuz Test Project

Austria 60, *102*, 104

B-52 bomber 22, 26, 30

Backfire bomber 42, 60

Ballistic Missile Early Warning System (BMEWS) 22–23

Baltic region 100, 108, 109, 111, 117

Ban the Bomb movement 29

Barre, Mohammed Siad 59

Beijing *105*–106

Belarus 115, 117

Berlin 38, 106, 107, 117

Berlin Wall 38, *107*, 108, 117

Bilak, Vasil 15, 16

Black Sea 92, 109, 112

BMEWS—see Ballistic Missile Early Warning System

Brandt, Willy 37–38, 116

Brazil 49

Brezhnev Doctrine 18

Brezhnev, Leonid 4, 8–9, 10, 13, 16, 18, 20, 34, 37, 38–39, 40, 41–42, 43, 44, 49, 51, 52, 57, 59–60, 65–66, 67, 76, 82, 83, 116, 117

broken arrow *30*, 118

Brown, Harold 24, 25, 29

Brzezinski, Zbigniew *51*, 53, 55, 57, 59, 63, 66, 67

Bucharest 109

Bulgaria 16, 108, 109, 117

Bush, George 90, 100, 102, 103–104, 107, 108, 109, 113, 115, 117

Campaign for Nuclear Disarmament (CND) 29

Camp David Accords 52

Canada 43, 120

capitalism 118

Caribbean Sea 80

Carter, Jimmy 4, 50, *51*–52, 53, 54, 55, 56, 57, 59–60, 62, 66, 67, 68, 72, *76*, 77, 78, 81, 116

Castro, Fidel 49, 108

Ceausescu, Nicolae 104, 109, 117

Central America 79, 80, 81, 108

Central Committee 7, 8

Central Intelligence Agency (CIA) 48, 67, 72, 88, 94, 103, 118

CFE treaty—see Conventional Forces in Europe treaty

Chamorra, Violeta 81

Charter 77, 53, 54–55

Chechnya 112

Chernenko, Konstantin 88, 90

Chernobyl power plant 95–96, 117

China 21, *31*, 37, 52, 56, 57, 63, 65, 67, 68, 76, 103, 105, 106, 116

China, Communist 37, 52, 68, *106*, 116

Chinese Communist party—see Communist party, Chinese

CIA—see Central Intelligence Agency

Clinton, Bill 104

CND—see Campaign for Nuclear Disarmament

Commonwealth of Independent States 115, 117

communism 14, 46, 69, 70, 71, 72, 91, 105, 108, 109, 115, 118

Communist party, Chinese 105, 106

Communist party, Czechoslovak 14, 15

Communist party, Polish 72, 73, 74

Communist party, Soviet 7–8, 9, 13, 18, 64, 83, 88, 90, 91, 92, 93, 109, 111, 112, 113, 120

Conference on Security and Cooperation 43

Contras *79*–80, 81, 117

Conventional Forces in Europe (CFE) treaty 112

Costa Rica 80

cruise missile 42, 56–57, 98, 99

Cuba 6, *31*, 48, 49, 58,59, 79, 87, 108

Cuban Missile Crisis 6, 20, 35, 41

Czechoslovak Communist party—see Communist party, Czechoslovak

Czechoslovakia 13–14, 15–*17*, 32, 53, 60, 69, 104, 108, 117

Czech Republic 14

democracy 14, 46, 52, 87, 106, 107, 109, 117, 118

Deng Xiaoping 105

détente 4, 9, 34, 37, 40, 41, 42–43, 45, 46, 48, 50, 54, 57, 59, 60, 64, 73, 118

Djibouti 59

Dobrynin, Anatoly 34–35, 36, 38, 44, 51

Dubcek, Alexander 14–15, 16, 17, 116

East Berlin 107

Eastern Europe 4, 13, 15, 20, 44, 69, 93, 100, 102, 103, 108, 109, 117

East Germany 15, 16, 37, 38, 68, 104–105, 106, 108, 110, 116, 117

Egypt 10, *11*, 12, 13, 40, 52, *76*, 116

Eisenhower, Dwight D. 9, 24

El Salvador 78, 79

England—see Great Britain

Estonia 100, 108, 110

Ethiopia *58*, 59

Europe 4, 13, 15, 20, 23, 44, 55, 56, 69, 81, 82, 87, 93, 94, 97, 99, 100, 102, 103, 108, 109, 112, 115, 117

Finland 35, *43*

FNLA—see National Front for the Liberation of Angola

Ford, Gerald 41, 42, *43*, 44, 48, 49, 50, 51, 60, 77, 116

France 12, 21, *31*, 68

Geneva 91, 116, 117

Geneva summit 91–92, 93, 117

Germany 15, 16, 17, 37, 38, 56, 57, 68, 104–105, 106, 108, 109, 110, 116, 117

glasnost 91, 100, 119

Gomulka, Wladyslaw 13, 15

Gorbachev, Mikhail 4, 35, 88, *90*, 91, 92–94, 95, *96*, 97, 98, 99–100, 102, 103, 104, 105, 106, 107, 108–109, 110, 111, 112–114, 115, 117, 119, 120

Gordievsky, Oleg 88
Great Britain 12, 21, 23, 29, 57, 65, 68, 90
Grenada 87, 88
Gromyko, Andrei 88
Guatemala 79
gulags 46, 54, 119

Haig, Alexander 78, 79
Havel, Vaclav 14, 17, 53, 108
Helsinki 35, *43*, 68
Helsinki Accords 43–44, 53, 54, 116
Helsinki Watch 53
Hitler, Adolf 17, 38
Ho Chi Minh 9
Honduras 79, 80
Honecker, Erich 65–66, 104–105, 106, 107
Horn of Africa—see Africa, Horn of
Hot Line 66, 119
human rights 4, 43–44, 46, 52, 53–55, 116
Hungary 16, 68, 83, 102, 103, 104, 108, 109
Hussein, Saddam 103, 104
hydrogen bomb 20–*21*, 22, 26, 29, *30*, 53, 119, 121

ICBM—see intercontinental ballistic missile
Iceland 96, 117
INF treaty—see Intermediate-range Nuclear Force treaty
intercontinental ballistic missile (ICBM) 20, 22, 23, *31*, 35, 39, 55, 84, 97, 119
Intermediate-range Nuclear Force (INF) treaty 56, 99, 117
Iran *31*, 52, *63*, 64, 66, 78, 80
Iran-Contra affair 78, 80
Iranian hostage crisis 52, 66, 77, 80, 116
Iraq 103–104, 117
iron curtain 102, 119
Israel 10, *11*, 12, 40–41, 43, 52, 54, 76, 116

Jackson, Henry "Scoop" 43, 60
Japan 22, *31*, 62
Jaruzelski, Wojciech 72, 73–74, 103
John Paul II, Pope *69*, 70
Johnson, Lyndon B. 9, 10, 32, 50, 116

Kabul *63*, 65, 66
KAL incident—see Korean Air Lines incident
Kennan, George 82
Kennedy, John F. 9, 24
Kennedy, Robert 35
KGB 7, 46, 64, 66, 68, 83, 88, 119
Khrushchev, Nikita 4, *6*–8, 9, 20, 21, 27, 35, 46, 116
Kissinger, Henry 32, 35, 36, 37, 38, 39, 40, 41–42, 49
Kohl, Helmut 110
Korean Air Lines (KAL) incident 86–87, 88
Koryagin, Anatoly 54
Kosygin, Aleksei 15, 32, 62, 116
Kremlin 38
Krenz, Egon 107
Kuwait 103–104, 117

Latin America 78, 121
Latvia 100, 108, 109, 111
Libya *31*, 94
Lithuania 100, 108, 109, 111
London 88
Luanda 49, 50

MAD—see mutual assured destruction
Malta 108, 117
Malta summit 108, 117
Managua 80
Mao Zedong 21, 106
massive retaliation 24, 120
McNamara, Robert 10, 24, 25–26, 32
Mediterranean Sea *11*, 12, 30, 108
Mengistu Haile Mariam 59
Middle East 10, *11*, 12, 40–41, 62, 67, 68, 80, 103
Minuteman 22
MIRV—see multiple independently targeted re-entry vehicle
Moldova 109
Moscow *7*–8, 12, 14, 16, 32, 34, 35, *36*, 37, 40, 41, 51, 53, 54, 59, 62, 67, 68, 76, 82, 83, 88, 93, 99, 102, 107, 108, 111, 113, 116, 117
MPLA—see Popular Movement for the Liberation of Angola
mujahedeen 62, 63–64, 65, *67*, 68, 78, 94, 95, 120
multiple independently targeted re-entry vehicle (MIRV) 32, 42, 56, 120

Munich 68, 69
mutual assured destruction (MAD) 25–26, 27, 29, 31–32, 84, 120
MX missile 60

Nasser, Gamal Abdel 10, 12–13
National Front for the Liberation of Angola (FNLA) 48, 49, *58*
National Security Council (NSC) 97
National Union for the Total Independence of Angola (UNITA) 48, 49, 50, *58*
NATO—see North Atlantic Treaty Organization
Nazis 17, 38
Nemeth, Miklos 102
neutron bomb 81–82, 120
New York City 82
Nicaragua 78–79, 80–81, 116, 117
Nixon, Richard 4, 32, 34, 36–37, 38–39, 40, 41, 51, 103, 116
No Cities/Counterforce 24
NORAD—see North American Air Defense Command
North American Air Defense Command (NORAD) 23, 120
North Atlantic Treaty Organization (NATO) 22, 35, 37, 55, 56, 87, 88, 110, 120
North Vietnam 9, 38
Novotny, Antonin 13, 14, 15
NSC—see National Security Council
nuclear weapons 4, 6, 7, 9, 20–21, 22, 23–24, 25–26, 27, 28, *29*–30, *31*, 32, 35–*36*, 38, 39, 41–42, 50, 51, 53, 55–57, 59–60, 78, 81–82, 84, 85, 86, 87, 91, 92, 93–94, 95, 97, 98, 99, 112, 115, 116, 118, 119, 120, 121

Olympic Games 68–69, 116
Ortega, Daniel 79, 81
Ostpolitik 38

Pakistan *31*, 63, 64–65, 66, 67, 82
Palomares 30
Panama 81
Paris 46
perestroika 91, 100, 104, 106, 108, 111, 120
Pershing II missile 56–57, 82, 99
Persian Gulf War 104
Poland 13, 15, 16, 38, 68, 69–70, 71, 72, 73, *74*, 103, 104, 108, 116, 117
Polaris missile 22, 27, 29

Polish Communist party—see Communist party, Polish

Polish First Army 74

Polish Homeland Army 74

Popular Movement for the Liberation of Angola (MPLA) 48–49, 50, *58*

Portugal *31*, 48, 49, 50

Prague *13, 17*

Prague Spring 14, 15, 16, 17, 116

Putin, Vladimir 112

Reagan, Ronald 4, 73, 76–78, 79, 80, 81, 82, 83, 84, 85, 86, 87, 88, 91–92, 93, 94, *96*, 97–99, 100, 102, 103, 115, 116, 117, 121

Red Sea *11*, 12, *58*

Regan, Donald 84, 93, 97

Reykjavik 96, 117

Reykjavik summit *96*–99, 117

Riga 111

Roman Catholic Church 70

Romania 104, 109, 117

Russia 46, 62, 83, 92, 110, 111, 112, 114–115, 117, 118

Russian Revolution 118

SAC—see Strategic Air Command

Sakharov, Andrei 53–54

SALT Accords—see Strategic Arms Limitation Talks Accords

SAM—see surface-to-air missile

Sandinistas 78–79, *80*, 81, 116

Savimbi, Jonas 50

SDI—see Strategic Defense Initiative

Sharansky, Natan—see Shcharansky, Anatoly

Shcharansky, Anatoly 54, 57, 100

Shevardnadze, Eduard 91, 110

Shultz, George 88, 90, 91, 97

Six-Day War 10, *11*, 12, 116

SLBM—see submarine-launched ballistic missile

socialism 6, 14, 16, 18, 107, 118, 121

Solidarity 71, *72*–73, 74, 103, 116, 117

Solzhenitsyn, Aleksandr 46

Somalia *58*, 59

Somoza, Anastasio 79

South Africa 49, *58*

Southeast Asia 10

South Korea 22, *31*

South Vietnam 9, 116

Soviet Communist party—see Communist party, Soviet

Soviet Union 4, 6, 8, 9–10, 12, 13, 14, 15, 16, 17, 18, 20, *21*, 23, 24, 25, 26, 27, 28, 29, 30, *31*, 32, 34, 35, 36, 37, 38, 39, 40–42, 43, 44–45, 46, 48, 49, 50, 52, 53, 54, 55, 56, 57, 58, 59, 60, 62, 63, 64, 66, 67–68, 69, 72, 73, 74, 76, 77, 78, 79, 82, 83, 84, 85, 86, 87, 88, 90, 91, 92, 93, 94, 95, 96, 97, 99–100, 103, 105, 106, 108, 109, 110, 111, 112, 113, 114, 115, 116, 117, 119, 120, 121

Afghanistan, role in 4, 9, 60, 62, 63, 64, 65–66, 67–68, 78, 82, 83, 94, 95, 116, 117, 120

Angola, role in 48–49, 50, 58, 116

Brezhnev Doctrine 18

China, relations with 21, 37, 106

civil defense 29, 118

collapse of 4, 93, 110, 111, 112, 113–115, 117

Communist party of 7–8, 9, 13, 18, 64, 83, 87, 90, 91, 92, 93, 109, 111, 112, 113, 120

Conventional Forces in Europe (CFE) treaty 112

Cuban Missile Crisis, role in 6, 20, 35

Czechoslovakia, role in 14, 15–17, 18, 32, 60, 69, 116

détente 4, 9, 34, 37, 40, 41, 42–43, 45, 46, 48, 50, 54, 57, 59, 60, 64, 73

Egypt, relations with 10, 12, 40

espionage 88

Germany, role in 38, 104, 106, 107, 110, 116

glasnost 91, 100, 119

gulags 46, 54, 119

Horn of Africa, role in 57, *58*, 59

human rights 4, 43–44, 46, 52, 53–54

Hungary, role in 68, 83, 102, 103

Intermediate-range Nuclear Force (INF) treaty 56, 99, 117

Korean Air Lines (KAL) incident 86–87

Middle East, role in 10, 12, 40–41, 103

Moscow 7–8, 12, 14, 16, 32, 34, 35, *36*, 37, 40, 41, 51, 53, 54, 59, 62, 67, 68, 76, 82, 83, 88, 92, 99, 102, 107, 108, 111, 113, 116, 117

Nicaragua, role in 79

Soviet Union continued

nuclear weapons development and use 4, 6, 7, 9, 20–21, 23, 24, 25, 26, 27, 29, 30, *31*, 32, 35–*36*, 38, 39, 41–42, 51, 53, 55–56, 57, 59–60, 82, 84, 85, 86, 87, 88, 91, 92, 93–94, 95, 97, 98, 99, 112, 115, 117, 121

perestroika 91, 100, 104, 106, 108, 111, 120

Poland, role in 13, 69, 70, 72, 73, 74

satellites of 4, 13–17, 18, 53, 54–55, 60, 68, 69–70, 71, 72, 73, 74, 83, 92, 102, 103, 104–105, 106–107, 108, 109, 110, 111, 116, 117

space program 39, 44–45, 48, 116

Strategic Arms Limitation Talks (SALT) 4, 32, 35–36, 37, 39, 42, 43, 44, 52, 55, 60, 67, 76, 116, 121

Strategic Arms Reduction Talks (START) 82, 108, 112, 117, 121

superpower, role as 4, 39, 40, 41, 44, 115

thermonuclear weapons development 20–21,53

U.S. relations with 4, 6, 9, 10, 24, 25, 26, 32, 34, 35–37, 38–39, 40–43, 44–45, 49, 50, 51, 52–53, 55, 56, 57, 59–60, 66, 67, 68–69, 76, 77, 78, 82, 84, 86, 87, 88, 90, 91–92, 96–100, 102, 103, 108, 110, 112, 113, 116, 117

Vietnam, involvement in 9–10

Virgin Lands 9

Warsaw Pact, role in 15, 44, 72, 106, 116

Spain 22, *30*, *31*, 81

SS-4 missile 56

SS-5 missile 56

SS-9 missile 31

SS-20 missile 55, 56, 82, 99

Stalin, Joseph 6, 7, 8, 46, 115

START—see Strategic Arms Reduction Talks

Star Wars—see Strategic Defense Initiative

Stinger missile 94, 95

Strategic Air Command (SAC) 22, 24, 26, 121

Strategic Arms Limitation Talks (SALT) I Accords 4, 32, 35–*36*, 37, 39, 43, 44, 55, 116, 121

Strategic Arms Limitation Talks (SALT) II Accords 39, 42, 43, 52, 60, 67, *76*, 116, 121

Strategic Arms Reduction Talks (START) 82, 108, 112, 117, 121

Strategic Defense Initiative (SDI) 4, 83, 84–86, 91–92, 97, 98, 99, 117

submarine-launched ballistic missile (SLBM) 22, 36, 39, 97, 121

submarines 22, 27, 28, 51, 121

Suez Canal 11, 12, 40

Suez Crisis 10

surface-to-air missile (SAM) 95, 121

Sweden 46, 96

Switzerland 46, 91, 116

Syria 11, 12, 40, 116

Taiwan 22, 68

Tajikistan 64

Taliban 65, 121

Tehran 52

Thatcher, Margaret 85, 90

thermonuclear weapons 20–21, 22, 26, 29, 30, 53, 119, 121

Tiananmen Square 105–106, 117

Titan II missile 22, 23–24

Turkey 6, 31, 36

Turkmenistan 64

U-2 spy plane 21

Ukraine 9, 35, 95, 109, 110, 115, 117

Ulbricht, Walter 15

UN—see United Nations

UNITA—see National Union for the Total Independence of Angola

United Arab Republic 12

United Nations (UN) 35, 50, 67, 82, 99, 103, 117

United States 4, 6, 9, 10, 12, 20, 21, 22, 23, 24, 25, 26, 28, 30, 31, 32, 34, 35, 36, 37, 38, 39, 40, 41, 42, 43, 44–45, 48, 49, 51, 52, 53, 55, 56, 57, 58, 59, 60, 62, 63, 67, 69, 73, 76, 77, 78, 79, 80, 81, 82, 84, 85, 86, 87, 88, 90, 91, 94, 95, 98, 99, 103, 107, 112, 114, 115, 116, 117, 119, 120, 121

Afghanistan, role in 4, 62, 63–64, 67, 78, 94, 95

Angola, role in 48, 49, 50, 116

China, relations with 21, 34, 37, 52, 57, 67, 76, 116

civil defense 28–29, 118

Conventional Forces in Europe (CFE) treaty 112

Cuban Missile Crisis, role in 6, 35

détente 4, 9, 34, 37, 40, 41, 42–43, 45, 46, 48, 50, 54, 57, 59, 60, 64, 73

United States continued

El Salvador, role in 78, 79

espionage 21, 28, 86, 87, 88, 94

Germany, role in 38

Grenada, role in 87, 88

Horn of Africa, role in 57, 58, 59

human rights 43–44, 53, 54

Intermediate-range Nuclear Force (INF) treaty 56, 99, 117

Iranian hostage crisis 52, 66, 77, 80, 116

Israel, relations with, 10, 12, 40, 41, 52, 76

massive retaliation 24, 120

Middle East, role in 10, 12, 40–41, 103

mutual assured destruction (MAD) 25–26, 27, 29, 31–32, 84, 120

Nicaragua, role in 78, 79–80, 81, 117

No Cities/Counterforce 24

North Atlantic Treaty Organization (NATO), role in 22, 55, 56, 87, 120

nuclear weapons development and use 4, 6, 9, 20, 21, 22, 23–24, 25–26, 27, 28, 29–30, 31, 32, 35–36, 38, 39, 41–42, 50, 51, 53, 55–57, 59–60, 78, 80–81, 82, 84, 85, 86, 87, 88, 91, 92, 93–94, 95, 97, 98, 99, 112, 115, 117, 118, 121

Pakistan, relations with 64, 66, 67

Soviet relations with 4, 6, 9, 10, 24, 25, 26, 32, 34, 35–37, 38–39, 40–43, 44–45, 49, 50, 51, 52–53, 55, 56, 57, 59–60, 66, 67, 68–69, 76, 77, 78, 82, 84, 86, 87, 88, 90, 91–92, 96–100, 102, 103, 108, 110, 112, 113, 116, 117

space program 39, 44–45, 48, 116

Strategic Arms Limitation Talks (SALT) 4, 32, 35–36, 37, 39, 42, 43, 44, 52, 55, 60, 67, 76, 116, 121

Strategic Arms Reduction Talks (START) 82, 108, 112, 117, 121

Strategic Defense Initiative (SDI) 4, 83, 84–86, 91–92, 97, 98, 99, 117

superpower, role as 4, 39, 40, 41, 44, 115

thermonuclear weapons development 22, 26, 30

Vietnam, involvement in 4, 9, 10, 34, 36, 38, 116

Washington, D.C. 34, 35, 56, 77

USSR—see Soviet Union

Uzbekistan 64

Vance, Cyrus 50, 51, 53, 63–64

Velvet Revolution 108, 117

Vienna 35, 60, 76

Vietnam 9, 34, 36, 37, 38, 116

Vietnam War 4, 34, 50, 64

Vilnius 111

Virgin Lands 9

Vladivostok 42, 51, 60, 116

Walesa, Lech 69, 70–71, 72, 73, 74, 103

Warsaw 13, 70, 74

Warsaw Pact 15, 16, 44, 64, 72, 106, 116

Washington, D.C. 34, 35, 56, 77, 99

Watergate scandal 39, 41

Weinberger, Caspar 78

West Berlin 38, 107

Western Europe 23, 82, 102

West Germany 37–38, 68, 104, 110, 117

Wojtyla, Karol—see John Paul II, Pope

World War I 73, 99

World War II 14, 17, 21, 25, 34, 38, 40, 44, 67, 77, 83, 109, 110, 115, 116, 117

Yeltsin, Boris 110, 111–112, 113, 114, 117

Yom Kippur War 40–41

Yugoslavia 109

$35.68

DATE			